STUDIES IN AMERICAN HISTORY

VII

THE COLOR PROBLEM
IN EARLY NATIONAL AMERICA
AS VIEWED BY JOHN ADAMS,
JEFFERSON AND JACKSON

BY

FREDERICK M. BINDER

1968

MOUTON

THE HAGUE · PARIS

LIBRARY OF CONGRESS CATALOG CARD NUMBER: 68-17871

Printed in The Netherlands by Mouton & Co., Printers, The Hague.

FOR TERIS

PREFACE

The race question poses one of the most difficult problems facing the leadership of our nation. Scarcely a day passes when the struggle to attain civil rights for the Negro is not vividly portrayed in our newspapers, on the radio and on television. Though less frequently publicized, the Indian too presents problems, ones which the federal government is even more clearly responsible for solving, in a legal as well as moral sense, than those of the Negro. For the national government has been the agency which has made and broken the treaties with the Indian's forebears, established the reservation upon which he likely lives today, and devised and revised those innumerable and largely unsuccessful plans for finding a place for his people in our society. Other races share some of the burdens of second class citizenship with the Indians and Negroes, but it is these two which have been with us the longest and which still present problems of the greatest difficulty.

Recognizing that any intelligent discussion of a contemporary problem should profit from examining the roots of the controversy, this work will investigate the color problem in the formative period of our nation as revealed in the thoughts and deeds of three outstanding political figures who rose to the office of President. The choice of John Adams, Thomas Jefferson, and Andrew Jackson has been based upon the desire to study the ideas of men who are clearly recognized as leaders of political movements, as well as being patriots, and to include individuals who are historically associated with each of the major sections of the nation as well as with the nation as a whole. The choice of men who achieved the Presidency presents an opportunity to observe the shaping of national policy where the Negro and Indian were concerned and an indication of the relationship between the personal views of these Presidents and the policies they advocated. The need for such a study is made evident by the fact that there is no single work devoted to the racial views of our early national leaders, nor have biographers done very much with the subject. It is also hoped that a broader understanding of the minds of three of the most distinguished Americans may be obtained.

In compiling data for this study, primary reliance has been placed upon the published collected writings of the three Presidents. In addition, biographical works, legislative records, local histories, monographs concerned with the Negro and Indian, administrative histories and periodicals have been utilized.

The choice of the term "color problem" is based upon the historical usage of the term "color" to denote non-whites in the United States. The government census reports throughout the period being discussed employed this word in presenting the totals of Negro and Indian population figures.

There are several people to whom I owe debts of gratitude. Professor Frederick D. Kershner, Jr., my advisor throughout the years as a doctoral candidate at Teachers College, Columbia University, provided the inspiration for my interest in intellectual history. His constructive advice, incisive criticism and patient understanding were major contributions to the completion of this study in its initial form as a doctoral dissertation (1962). Professors Erling Hunt and Alice Spieseke of Teachers College offered helpful suggestions on numerous occasions. Professor Morton M. Rosenberg of Ball State University and Professor Merl Reed of Georgia State University were kind enough to read sections of the work and to contribute both encouragement and many valuable editorial comments. More than any other person, I am indebted to my wife, Teris, who brought to our marriage love, patience, typing skill, editorial advice and a copy of *Roget's International Thesaurus*.

The City College of New York   Frederick M. Binder
October, 1967

TABLE OF CONTENTS

CHAPTER I

JOHN ADAMS AND THE NEGRO

The views of John Adams on any national problem warrant close attention by those interested in the climate of thought in early national America. In New England and particularly among the most influential Federalists from that section, no political figure was of greater stature. As a Founding Father, diplomat, party leader, Vice President and President, he had innumerable opportunities to offer leadership in the formation and excution of national policy. As confidant of national and local leaders he was in a position to influence and be influenced by their views. As a man whose life spanned ninety-one years he was able to observe and comment upon some of the most significant events in United States history. To the extent that he influenced his son, John Quincy Adams, his presence was felt in national deliberations a generation after his death.

For the most part the biographers of John Adams have, by dint of omission, left the impression that the color problem was virtually foreign to Adams' environment, thoughts and deeds. The absence of "Negro", "slavery", and "Indian" from most indices may very well be the result of a failure to find in Adams' writings clearly defined and oft repeated views regarding these subjects. Sparse as such references may be, they can be found here and there among his letters, diary, addresses, autobiography and other published works. A study of these, when set against attitudes and practices in the New England of Adams' prime years, can contribute a great deal towards a formulation of his views of the problem.

Adams' writings reveal that he either had little contact with Negroes or displayed no particular interest in their condition in the years prior to the Revolution. In 1766 one finds the first mention of the Negro in his diary. Taken out of context, it might easily be construed as a rather glowing tribute to the Negro and a condemnation of slavery. Adams spoke of a certain group of Negroes as having "more of the Spirit of Liberty" than their masters and condemned the latter for their "mean timid resignation" to slavery. But these were not Massachusetts slaves and masters, nor even those of the Southern colonies of whom he wrote in the private confines of his diary. Adams' statements were a subordinate part of his vitriolic censure of the West Indian planters for their failure to join the protest movement against the Stamp Act.[1]

This was the only time the Negro entered into Adams' political expressions before 1776. However, Adams the lawyer and private citizen recorded a few personal experiences with members of that race. As a lawyer in 1766, he observed and expressed interest in a case involving a mulatto woman who was suing a white man for having restrained her movements. "This is called suing for liberty; the first action that ever I knew of the sort, though I have heard there have been many."[2] In 1768 he was "accidentally" engaged in the defense of a master against a suit brought by a slave. He won the case.[3] In referring to both cases Adams displayed no more than a professional, legal interest in the participants.

It was not until the decade of the seventies that Adams recorded in his diary instances of personal contact with Negroes outside the court room. As his legal practice and interest in politics increased, so also did his travels and social obligations. Here and there he noted a dinner served by a Negro, along with a description of each course and each guest. The fact that the Negro was a slave does not appear to have troubled him. In one instance he noted an after-dinner discussion at the home of his friend Dr. Cooper. During the course of the conversation the host referred to the wisdom of his Negro servant. "Dr. Cooper quoted another proverb from his Negro, Glasgow . . . and then told us another instance of Glasgow's intellect, of which I had before thought him entirely destitute."[4] A month later, on June 17, 1771, Adams recorded the only account to be found in his diary of a personal conversation with a Negro:

Rode with King; a deputy sheriff, who came to meet the Judge, into Salem; put up at Goodhues. The Negro that took my horse soon began to open his heart;—he did not like the people of Salem; wanted to be sold to

[1] L. H. Butterfield (ed.), *Diary and Autobiography of John Adams* (Cambridge, Harvard University Press, 1961), I, 285.

[2] *Ibid.*, 321 (November 5, 1766).

[3] *Ibid.*, III, 289. Adams referred to this case in his autobiography, begun on October 5, 1802.

[4] *Ibid.*, II, 140 (May 14, 1771).

Captain John Dean, of Boston; he earned two dollars in a forenoon, and did all he could to give satisfaction, but his mistress was cross, and said he did not earn salt to his porridge, etc., and would not find him clothes, etc. Thus I find discontents in all men;—the black thinks his merit rewarded with ingratitude, and so does the white; the black estimates his own worth and the merit of his services higher than anybody else, so does the white. This flattery, fond opinion of himself, is found in every man.[5]

These two accounts are significant because they appear to be the only references Adams made to particular Negroes. Even more interesting, in both cases Adams made value judgements, commenting on the intellect of Glasgow in the first entry and the character of the Salem slave in the second. However, in neither instance does it appear that Adams was particularly interested in commenting on Negro slavery or on Negro attributes in general. On the contrary, these seem only two more examples of the manifold comments Adams made throughout his life concerning collective Man and individual men. In the statement regarding his Salem adventure Adams attached the characteristics of one Negro slave to all members of that race and compared the "black" to the "white". But what is apparent and significant is that Adams' intention was to utilize this experience to emphasize the egotism "found in every man"; the "discontents [found] in all men". Thus, the only comparison between Negro and white found among Adams' writings emphasizes their *similarity*, albeit in terms of mutual weaknesses, and also to their *unity* as men.

These few remarks concerning the Negro indicate that lawyer Adams considered this race and the institution of slavery to have been no more than of passing interest, certainly not subjects important enough to warrant either a strong public or private stand.

The coming of the Revolution marked the emergence of John Adams as a national figure. Though rooted in Massachusetts soil and sent to the Continental Congress to represent the interests of his native state, his responsibilities and outlook gradually broadened so that today he is honored as a Founding Father and early national leader. During the years in which Adams was actively involved in the government his view of the Negro quite naturally expanded. Various aspects of slavery appeared as political issues both in the struggle with Great Britain and the debates relative to the formation of a union of the thirteen colony-states. The political mind of John Adams could not shut itself off completely from these issues, nor

[5] *Ibid.*, 36.

could Adams, the intellectual, ignore those who insisted that the existence of Negro slavery was contrary to the declarations of political and moral rights promulgated by the Revolution.

Adams' statements regarding public policy in which the Negro was involved seem to follow a definite pattern. They indicate that he looked upon slavery as an instrument of political infighting, to be used or avoided depending on its relation to other interests with which he was more concerned. In April of 1776, in the Continental Congress, Adams found himself strongly supporting the demands of his fellow Massachusetts delegates, as well as those from Maryland and Virginia, that the slave trade be abolished. "There is one Resolution which I will not omit — 'Resolved, that no Slaves be imported into any of the thirteen Colonies.' " [6]

It was not difficult for Northerner and Southerner to stand together as Americans in a humane expression of contempt for the abominable trade. In doing so they were at the same time repeating an attack on George III. The attitude that the slave trade was foisted upon the Colonies by Britain was shared by many Americans. The inclusion of a non-importation of slaves clause in the Association indicates that a majority in Congress felt that the slave trade most benefited the mother country, and that any action which restricted it would damage Britain's economy. [7]

Three months after Mr. Adams' verbal attack on the slave trade, he spoke to the Continental Congress of the similarities between the contributions and conditions of the Southern slave and the free laborer in the North. These words could never be construed as the expression of an anti-slavery advocate, nor as an attack by an American upon the misdeeds of the mother country. Here John Adams argued as a Massachusetts delegate in defense of the interests of his section against what he saw as a threat emanating from the South. Thomas Jefferson noted the speech:

Mr. John Adams observed that the numbers of people were taken by this article as an index of the wealth of the state and not as subjects of taxation, that as to this matter it was of no consequence by what you called your people, whether by that of freemen or of slaves; that in some countries the labouring poor were called freemen, in other they were called

[6] *Ibid.*, III, 377. These sentiments were recalled by Adams in his autobiography.
[7] Henry Steele Commager (ed.), *Documents of American History* (New York, Appleton-Century-Crofts, Inc., 1963), p. 85. Association established by Act of the Continental Congress, Philadelphia, October 20, 1774.

slaves; but that the difference as to the state was imaginary only. What matters is whether a landlord employing ten labourers in his farm, gives them annually as much money as will by them the necessaries life, or gives them those necessaries at short hand. The ten labourers add as much wealth annually to the state, increase its exports as much in one case as the other ... therefore the state in which are the labourers called freemen should be taxed no more than that in which are those called slaves.[8]

Adams went on to stress similarities between the free laborer and slave, stating that the conditions of the Northern fisherman were as "painful abject as that of slaves" and concluded "that a slave may indeed from custom of speech be more properly called the wealth of his master, than the free labourer might be called the wealth of his employer; but ... as to the state both were equally its wealth, and should therefore equally add to the quota of its tax."[9]

Just as Adams was willing on the one hand to attack the slave trade and on the other to emphasize the similarities of slave and free labor, he was determined, when he thought it necessary, to help muffle the slavery issue. In 1777 Adams, in agreement with his friend James Warren concerning an emancipation bill before the Massachusetts legislature, wrote, "The Bill for freeing the Negroes, I hope, will sleep for a time. We have cause enough of Jealousy, Discord and Division and this Bill will certainly add to the Number."[10] The concern shown by Adams and Warren was reflected in the Massachusetts legislature, where the bill was put on the table.[11]

Serving as a delegate to the Continental Congress, as has been noted, resulted at times in conflicts between Adams' obligation to serve the interests of his state and the desire to foster national unity. However, in the decade of the eighties he was able to serve both causes equally well in his capacities as delegate to the peace negotiations in Paris and minister to Great Britain. Massachusetts could well be pleased with his efforts on behalf of the fishing interests at the peace conference. The qualms of some Southerners regarding Adams'

[8] Julian P. Boyd (ed.), *The Papers of Thomas Jefferson* (Princeton, N.J., Princeton University Press, 1952-), I, 321.
[9] *Ibid.*
[10] *Warren-Adams Letters* (Boston, Massachusetts Historical Society, 1917), I, 339. This letter, dated July 7, 1777, was in response to Warren's sentiments of concern expressed in a letter to Adams dated June 22, 1777. *Ibid.*, p. 335.
[11] James Ford, "Social Conditions and Social Changes, 1789-1820", *Commonwealth History of Massachusetts*, Albert Bushnell Hart (ed.), (New York, The States History Company, 1927-1928), I, 508.

willingness to work for their section must have been quickly put aside.[12]
Any personal repugnance to slavery which Adams might have entertained at this time was not reflected in his diplomatic dealings. In
Paris in 1782, he joined his fellow commissioners in demanding that
Britain cease further carrying off of Negroes. To Secretary Livingston
he wrote, ". . . there is every argument of national honor, dignity of
the state, public and private justice and humanity, for us to insist
upon a compensation for all plate, negroes, rice, and tobacco stolen,
and houses consumed, as there is for them to demand compensation
to the tories."[13] In London, three years later, Adams persisted in
presenting American demands for reparation payments covering the
slaves carried off in the late war.[14]

It is ironic that the year 1785 should present us with this picture
of Adams the diplomat working tirelessly for such reparations and
also reveal him reading and applauding Jefferson's attack on slavery
in *Notes on the State of Virginia*. "The Passages upon slavery are
worth Diamonds. They will have more effect than Volumes written
by mere Philosophers."[15] However, whereas Adams' diligent efforts
in London provide a measure of his dedication to the nation, no
words or deeds with which one can easily gauge the nature or
intensity of his opposition to slavery follow this brief, enthusiastic
response to Jefferson's work. Searching among the published writings
of Adams for statements concerning the Negro, one finds a void from
1787 to 1801. Concerning the debates over slavery in the national
and state constitutional conventions, Adams, still in London, apparently remained silent. The Three-Fifths Compromise and the twenty-
year hands-off policy toward the slave trade removed slavery as a
national political issue during the remaining years of Adams' active
career in public life, and he obviously felt no desire to disturb the

[12] Elbridge Gerry informed Adams that some Southern members opposed his
nomination as minister on the grounds that he had expressed views against the
slave trade and would not exert himself "to obtain restitution of the Negroes taken
and detained from them in Violation of the Treaty". Edmund C. Burnett (ed.),
Letters of Members of the Continental Congress (Washington, D.C., The Carnegie
Institution of Washington, 1921-1936), VIII, 39-40, February 24, 1785.
[13] Charles Francis Adams (ed.), *The Works of John Adams* (Boston, Little,
Brown and Company, 1856), VIII, 7 (November 8, 1782).
[14] Adams reported these fruitless efforts to Jay in letters dated the 15th and
21st of October, 1785. U.S. Dept. of State, *The Diplomatic Correspondence of
the United States of America, 1783-1789* (Washington, F. P. Blair, 1833-34), II,
479, 483-91.
[15] Lester J. Cappon (ed.), *The Adams-Jefferson Letters* (Chapel Hill, The University of North Carolina Press, 1959), I, 21, To Thomas Jefferson (May 22, 1785).

peace. Adams' attack on the slave trade in 1776 appears to have been the only public expression during his active political years in which he made a judgement concerning an aspect of slavery. His writings indicate that the statement and its isolated character fairly well reflect the limited range and intensity of his views toward slavery. There are three references in Adams' writings during the Revolutionary and Confederation periods which confirm this. Each reflects a mildly hostile view toward the institution, but the emphasis in each case is upon the perpetrators of the evil, the slave owner and trader, rather than upon the victim, the Negro.

The first of these references appears in his diary entry of February 23, 1777. Here he commented on the division of labor in Maryland and, since no views concerning the treatment or condition of the Negroes were offered, the reader receives the impression that Adams felt that the worst aspects of slavery were its effects upon the morals of the owners. These men he described as so contemptuous of Negroes, laborers, and tradesmen that they considered themselves "a distinct order of Beings". He found their sons, discouraged from engaging in any form of worthwhile endeavor, being brought up "in Idleness or what is worse in Horse Racing, Cockfighting and Card Playing".[16] It appears that Adams felt that slavery was a devilish tool which led men to indulge in further vices. This view is fortified by the second reference, a notation in Adams' handwriting on the cover page of a collection of abolition essays by Count Sarsefield: "Aut Sarsefieldii aut Diaboli." [17] Adams' failure to take a strong public or personal stand against slavery indicates that this admonition was directed toward those who dealt directly with slaves. They, and not Adams, would have to choose between abolition and the Devil.

In the third reference, a letter written to Granville Sharp, Adams took advantage of the Barbary pirate problem to engage in a bit of moral preachment. He stated that in making slaves of prisoners of war the pirates were merely employing a principle accepted in the slave trade. "I expect that one part of Africa will avenge upon my fellow citizens the injury they do to another by purchasing their prisoners." [18]

Negro slavery reappeared in Adams' writings during the years following his retirement. There is no evidence, however, of a differ-

[16] Butterfield, *Diary and Autobiography*, II, 261.
[17] *Ibid.*, III, 16. The editor found the notation among the Adams papers filed at 1782-1783.
[18] C. F. Adams, *Works*, VIII, 388-89 (March 8, 1786).

ent approach to the problem. Again we find a repetition of the early pattern of employing or playing down the slavery issue as it served other interests, while making frequent assertions of personal abhorrence of the institution.

In a letter addressed to George Churchman and Jacob Lindley shortly after his defeat at the hands of Jefferson and the Republicans, Adams summed up virtually every sentiment regarding Negro slavery to be found elsewhere in his writings. Here are included declarations of personal disapproval of slavery, concern for the welfare of the masters, and fear of upheaval as well as a relegation of the problem to a secondary position. "Although I have never sought popularity by any animated speeches or inflammatory publications against the slavery of the black, my opinion against it has always been known, and my practise has been so conformable to my sentiments that I have always employed free men; both as domestics and laborers and never did I own a slave." [19]

Adams' expression of distaste is obviously accurate. However, one wonders how this silence could have made his alleged anti-slavery views "well-known", or have influenced public opinion to any extent. In the elections of 1796 and 1800 Adams received his greatest Southern support from the counties of highest slave concentration.[20] Despite their apparent dislike for Jeffersonian Republicanism, it is difficult to imagine that these slaveholders would support a man whom they thought firmly opposed to slavery outside the limits of his own four walls.

The Southern Federalist, who might have felt uncomfortable upon reading the initial paragraph of the letter to Churchman and Lindley, could soon relax upon continuing. "The abolition of slavery must be gradual and accomplished with much caution and circumspection. Neither Mr. Mifflin nor yourselves, I presume, would be willing to venture an exertion which would probably excite insurrections among the blacks to rise against their masters, and imbue their hands in innocent blood." Adams then went on to state that there were more important evils in our country, and that slavery was diminishing anyway. "These vices and miseries deserve the serious and compassionate consideration of friends, as well as the slave trade and degraded state of the blacks." [21]

[19]   Ibid., IX, 92 (January 24, 1801).
[20]   Manning J. Dauer, The Adams Federalists (Baltimore, The Johns Hopkins Press, 1953), p. 18.
[21]   C. F. Adams, Works, IX, 92-93.

Though Adams did not specify the vices to which he was referring, it may be assumed that he considered such things as the inhumane treatment of criminals and the insane to be at least as reprehensible as the existence of slavery, which was after all, in his opinion, diminishing. The proponents of emancipation found no willing and eager ally in the President about to retire. The most he could offer was that he would "always be ready to cooperate . . . as far as my means and opportunities can reasonably be expected to extend".[22]

Adams' interest in public affairs remained strong after his retirement to Quincy. As had been the case in earlier years, while showing an unwillingness to take a clear stand on Negro slavery, he did not hesitate at times to use the fact of its existence to advance a cause he considered important. Among the convictions he held dear, and continued to promote, was that "property has been, is, and, everlastingly will be, a natural and unavoidable cause of aristocracy".[23] In discussing this principle with John Taylor of Caroline, Adams employed the Negro to illustrate a point:

Suppose Congress should, at one vote, or by one act, declare all the negroes in the United States free, in imitation of that great authority, the French sovereign legislature, what would follow: Would the democracy, nine in ten, among the negroes, be gainers? Would not the most shiftless among them be in danger of perishing for want . . . go back to their masters, best of them work at horrible jobs, become squatters, incorporate with Indians, commit crimes in bands. . . . Will the poor simple, democratical part of the people gain any happiness by such rash revolution?[24]

John Taylor and Messrs. Churchman and Lindley could have had few doubts from the letters they received that Adams was opposed to immediate emancipation by legislative action. The danger to life and property was too high a price to pay.

The Missouri crisis once more illustrated that the slavery issue was also a danger to the maintenance of the Union. As in the case of the emancipation bill in 1777, Adams could not condone any action which might threaten national unity. He feared that "another Hamilton another Burr might rend this mighty fabric in twain".[25] During these troubled times Adams again wrote of his abhorrence of slavery, his sympathy with fellow Americans from the South and called for

22 *Ibid.*
23 *Ibid.*, VI, 512, To John Taylor of Caroline (April 15, 1814).
24 *Ibid.*, 511-12 (April 15, 1814).
25 *Ibid.*, X, 386, To Thomas Jefferson (December 18, 1819).

"some good neutral way or other ... to untie this very intricate knot".[26]

On February 3, 1821, Adams wrote on the slavery problem in a letter to Thomas Jefferson. In it he provides the essence of what appears to have consistently been his political approach to the issue:

Slavery in this Country I have seen hanging over it like a black cloud for half a century. ... I have been so terrified with this Phenomenon that I constantly said in former times to the Southern Gentlemen, I cannot comprehend this object; I must leave it to you. I will vote for forcing no measure against your judgement.[27]

Adams could offer no solution; no immediate gesture like tabling an emancipation bill was possible in 1821. He left it to God "and his agents in posterity". He freely admitted that he had "none of the genius of Franklin to invent a rod to draw from the cloud its Thunder and lightning".[28]

In 1819 Adams had written to Robert J. Evans expressing once again a hatred of slavery and a desire for eventual emancipation coupled with the inevitable concern for the slaveholders "who are so unfortunate as to be surrounded with these fellow creatures, by heredity descent, or by any other means without their own fault." He went on to speak of slavery as John Adams, private citizen:

I have through my whole life, held the practise of slavery in such abhorance, that I have never owned a negro or any other slave, though I have hired for many years in times, when the practise was not disgraceful, when the best men in my vicinity thought it was not inconsistent with their character, and when it has cost me thousands of dollars for the labor and subsistence of free men, which I might have saved by the purchase of negroes at times when they were very cheap.[29]

There seems no reason to challenge Adams' honesty in thus reiterating his personal distaste for slavery. It is equally probable that Adams considered the question to be overwhelming a matter of individual morals and the individual right to control property. Personal feeling was of no significance, weighed against property rights, so basic to

[26] L. J. Cappon, *Adams-Jefferson Letters*, II, 561, To Thomas Jefferson (February 21, 1820).
[27] *Ibid.*, 571.
[28] *Ibid.* For an analysis of John Adams' views of slavery as indicated by his reaction to the Missouri Crisis see John R. Howe, Jr., "John Adams's Views of Slavery", *Journal of Negro History*, XLIX (July, 1964), 201-06.
[29] C. F. Adams, *Works*, X, 380 (June 8, 1819).

the preservation of an orderly society. From his earliest days in Boston Adams had been friendly with slave owners and had been served by their Negroes. There is no indication that he tried to impose his personal position on slavery on anyone else, and it is likely that he felt no invidual or government should take comparabe action.

Adams' use of the Negro slave in Salem to illustrate propensities common to "every man", and the fact that racist thought was absent from his statements regarding the dangerous consequences of immediate emancipation, lead one to suspect that he did not consider the Negro to belong to an inferior race. However, there is no evidence that he gave this question serious attention. Indeed it appears that Adams' admitted distaste for slavery was conditioned much more by concern for the white than for the Negro. His statements regarding the Maryland planters and Count Sarsefield's abolition tract, his activities in the Continental Congress and as a diplomat, and the letters addressed to Taylor, Churchman and Lindley, Evans, and Jefferson reflect concern primarily for the life and morals of the slave traders and slave owners, the defense of property, the welfare of his state and the unity of the nation. Within the realm of Adams' private life and mind, moral considerations regarding slavery were evidently of real importance. In the arena of public affairs, however, Adams appeared to have been guided chiefly by what was politically expedient.

Nevertheless there are two key facts which cannot help but cast doubt upon, or at least weaken, this interpretation of John Adams' ideas about the Negro and slavery. In the first place, it is quite clear that Adams said very little on the subject and did not like to talk about it, unlike some of his famous contemporaries and most of his successors on the political scene. This is all the evidence Adam has given us, but is it sufficient to justify the conclusions reached? Secondly, one cannot help but be struck by the sharp contrast between the views of John Adams, as here presented, and those generally associated with his son and President, John Quincy Adams. Did the son repudiate the father, or have the ideas and attitudes of the father been distorted and misrepresented? These are questions which do not arise with either Jefferson or Jackson, and which would seem to require special treatment. The answer, if there is one, must surely be found in setting the two Adamses against their common New England environment, and determining therefrom the extent to which they merely reflected common attitudes, as distinguished from leading and changing public opinion through strongly held and expressed ideas of their own.

Negro slaves appeared early in Massachusetts and their status was acknowledged in the colony's first code of laws. In 1641, Article 91 of the *Body of Liberties* stated:

> There shall never be any bond slaverie, villenage or captives amongst us unless it be lawful captives taken in just warres, and such strangers as willingly sell themselves or are sold to us, and these shall have all the liberties and Christian usages which the law of God established in Israel concerning such persons doeth morally require. This exempts more from servitude who shall be Judged thereto by Authorities.[30]

Thus, sanctioned by Mosaic law, slavery took root in Massachusetts. In 1676 Edmund Randolph recorded "not above two hundred slaves in the colony and those were brought from Guinea and Madagascar." [31] In 1698 the roots were nourished by an act of the General Court declaring that the children of slaves were slaves.[32] The Negro population of the Bay Colony grew from an estimated 2600 in 1735 to 4000 in 1750. The first U. S. census listed 5463 colored people in Massachusetts. However, a comparison of these figures with estimates of the total Massachusetts population of 145,000 in 1735, 200,000 in 1755, and a census count of 378,787 in 1790, demonstrates that the Negro never constituted more than a small minority in the state.[33]

As Robert E. Brown has pointed out in his work, *Middle Class Democracy and the Revolution in Massachusetts*, slavery in Massachusetts did not function as a barometer of class society. From the examples he offers of slaveowners who had no real estate and whose total estates were minuscule, it appears that ownership of slaves was not a mark of wealth in that state.[34] There are no figures available

---

[30]   Cited in James Ford, "Social Life", *Commonwealth History of Massachusetts*, I, 269.

[31]   *Ibid.*

[32]   Allyn Barley Forbes, "Social Life in Town and Country 1689-1763", *Commonwealth History of Massachusetts*, II, 262.

[33]   Dept. of Commerce and Labor, Bureau of the Census, *A Century of Population Growth, 1790-1900* (Washington, Government Printing Office, 1909), pp. 5, 47. Included in the total of "colored" in the first U.S. census were 800 Indians.

[34]   Robert E. Brown, *Middle-Class Democracy and the Revolution in Massachusetts, 1691-1780* (Ithaca, Cornell University Press, 1955), p. 19.

as to the percentage of Negroes, slave or free, who worked on farms, in the trades or as domestics. However, in the small farm and mercantile economy of Massachusetts, slavery was hardly necessary for economic wellbeing.

In his history of the Congregationalist Church Leonard Bacon asserted, "With reference to the subject of slavery, also, the record of the primeval Congregationalists was wholly noble. The unbroken succession of protests and deeds against slavery has often been recorded...." [35] There is no indication, however, that more than a sprinkling of the clergy of colonial Massachusetts made their pulpits available for the cause of emancipation. More indicative is the fact that the laws establishing and controlling slavery were passed during a period when theological influence was still a strong factor in the legislature. One of the heroes mentioned by Bacon as being a foe of slavery was Samuel Sewall, whose *Selling of Joseph* employed natural rights philosophy in arguing against the institution. "Originally, and naturally, there is no such thing as Slavery." [36] Cotton Mather, also referred to by Bacon, saw to it in 1700 that Sewall's book was published. Nevertheless this same Mather, upon reaching maturity, purchased a slave and presented it as a gift to his father.[37]

The laws passed by the General Court and decrees issued by the Court of General Session in the early eighteenth century indicate no attempt to eliminate slavery, although they do show a desire to limit its expansion and control its effects. In 1705 three rulings reflecting this attitude were handed down by the legislature and court. An attempt was made to discourage the importation of Negroes by levying a duty of four pounds a head on those brought into the colony and not re-exported. An act to prevent mixed issue provided that any Negro having sexual relations with a white person would be sold out of the colony. Mixed marriages were prohibited, and a stiff fine was to be imposed on any minister performing such an act. The Court of General Session directed that Indians, Negroes, mulatto servants and slaves be kept off the streets after dark.[38]

The city which was to become an abolition center in the mid-

[35] Leonard W. Bacon, *The Story of the Churches, The Congregationalist* (New York, The Baker and Taylor Co., 1904), p. 207.
[36] Cited in Forbes, "Social Life", *Commonwealth History of Massachusetts*, II, 264.
[37] F. J. Stimson, "Massachusetts in Literature", *Commonwealth History of Massachusetts*, I, 374.
[38] Forbes, "Social Life", *Commonwealth History of Massachusetts*, II, 262-63.

nineteenth century appears to have been fearful of the color problem in the 1720's. Boston at this time directed its attention not to the effects of slavery on the Negro but to the effects of the Negro on the peace and safety of the general population. In 1723 the Town Meeting voted to recommend to the General Court an act for the restraint of Indians, Negroes and mulattoes. Such persons were to receive no visits from slaves under penalty of fine, imprisonment and whipping. They might possess no firearms or ammunition, nor were they to be allowed to sell "Strong drink, cake, or any other Provisions" on training days. It was further recommended that these people should bind out their children at four years of age to some English master. If they were found in possession of any stolen property or property of a slave, they should not only be whipped and be forced to make restitution, but be expelled from the colony, liable to life imprisonment if they returned. They were to be forbidden to gather together on the streets. Assault was to be punished by transportation. As a crowning touch Negroes and Indians were to be required to stay indoors when fires broke out. Unsupported testimony offered by Negroes and Indians was not to be acceptable. To encourage white interest in the enforcement of the provisions it was provided that half the fines and forfeitures under the regulations should go to the informer.[39] On June 21, 1773, the legislature passed the above recommendations hoping to prevent the "many mischievous Practises which the Indians, Negroes and mulattoes have of late in a most audacious manner to the Great Disturbance and grievous Damage of His Majesty's Good Subjects, more especially in the Town of Boston addicted themselves unto." [40]

Thus it appears likely that the Boston in which John Adams grew to political maturity was a town in which more concern was directed toward controlling the activities of the free people of color than challenging the existence of slavery. There were not many Negroes in Boston in Adams' day — the census of 1790 listed 761 colored inhabitants out of a total population of 18,038.[41] It is quite likely that this lover of order was, like his fellow citizens, more easily upset by the unruly behavior of free Negroes than by the polite, well supervised domestic slaves of his friends.

[39] Cited in Sherwin L. Cook, "Boston: The Eighteenth Century Town", *Commonwealth History of Massachusetts*, II, 227-28.
[40] *Journal of the House of Representatives of Massachusetts, 1723-1724* (Boston, Massachusetts Historical Society, 1924), V, 36, 48.
[41] Bureau of the Census, *A Century of Population Growth*, p. 84.

Adams' views of the Negro and slavery appear to have been shaped to some extent by brief, indirect encounters with that race. In only one instance did he record a detailed conversation with a Negro. Adams was probably too busy to give the relatively few Negroes of Boston much attention, unless their own initiative happened to attract it. Such was the case in Salem and also at Dr. Cooper's home. Such may very well have been the case when Boston's colored population became unruly. In 1774 Abigail Adams called the attention of her husband to a "conspiracy of the negroes" in Boston. The Negroes, it seems, offered their service as soldiers to the governor in return for a promise to liberate them. Mrs. Adams clearly stated her reaction to these activities. "I wish most sincerely that there was not a slave in the province. It always appeared a most inequitous scheme to me — to fight ourselves for what we are daily robbing and plundering from those who have as good a right to freedom as we have. You know my mind upon the subject." [42]

Adams answered this letter without commenting on the above incident. There is no evidence that he shared his wife's strong views regarding freedom for the Negro and concern with their lot. Indeed, if the views expressed in his letter to John Taylor of Caroline, written in 1814, in any way approached his concept of what freeing the slaves would mean in 1774, we may conclude that he differed quite radically with his wife on this point.

If Adams' political home, Boston, offered him little opportunity for direct contact with the Negro, it is doubtful whether his domestic environment in Braintree (later incorporated as part of Quincy) provided any contact at all. In only one of the various histories of Braintree and Quincy is there a reference to Negroes. Daniel Munro Wilson's work states that Colonel Edmund Quincy, in 1695, had three Negro slaves.[43] Adams attended the Congregationalist church of Mr. Lemuel Briant. If slavery was a topic of the pulpit, Adams never mentioned it in reminiscences of church-going found in his autobiography or other published writings, nor is the subject mentioned in the few available published works of Mr. Briant. These

---

[42] L. H. Butterfield (ed.), *Adams Family Correspondence* (Cambridge, The Belknap Press of Harvard University Press, 1965), I, 161-62, September 22, 1774.
[43] Daniel Munro Wilson, *Where American Independence Began. Quincy, Its Famous Group of Patriots; Their Deeds, Homes, and Descendents* (Boston and New York, Houghton, Mifflin and Co., 1902), p. 154.

appear to be primarily concerned with sinful men and a harsh God.[44]

Not until the conflict with Great Britain was Massachusetts forced to deal more directly with slavery. The slave trade was tied to the larger issues of colonial commerce, and there were those who, like Abigail Adams, questioned the compatibility of the various humanitarian expressions of the American colonists with the existence of slavery. However, events indicate that John Adams in his approach to the slavery issue was very much a Massachusetts man. His state did not rush into emancipation during the Revolutionary period. In 1777 the legislature tabled a bill to prevent "The Practice of holding persons in slavery" after hearing arguments similar to those expressed by James Warren and John Adams.[45] Slavery was never legislated out of existence. Article One of the Massachusetts Constitution of 1780 is generally credited for eliminating slavery in its declaration that "all men are born free and equal".[46] However, as late as March 15, 1781, the *Continental Journal* advertised a "likely Negro Wench" for sale.[47] It is probable that the state supreme court ruling in 1783, upholding a Worcester court's decision which declared Negroes free on the basis of the state constitution, sounded slavery's final knell.[48] In the 1790 census Massachusetts was the only state which reported no slaves within its boundaries.

On this issue the people of Massachusetts, whether in legislature assembled or acting as individuals, in most cases were not prone to force their practices or opinions on others. During the convention held to ratify the federal constitution, sentiment was expressed for an anti-slavery clause to be inserted into the document. The proponents of such a clause were decidedly in the minority. Speaking against such action were men like William Dawes, who stated:

The members of the southern states like ourselves, have their prejudices. It would not do to abolish slavery by an act of Congress, in a moment, and so destroy what our southern brethren consider a property. But we may

[44] Lemuel Briant, *The Absurdity of Blasphemy* (Boston, Green, 1749, 31 pages); Lemuel Briant, *Some More Friendly Remarks* (Boston, Green, 1751, 35 pages).
[45] Ford, "Social Conditions and Social Changes", *Commonwealth History of Massachusetts*, I, 508.
[46] Cited in Arthur R. Curnick, "Social Life in the Revolutionary Period", *Commonwealth History of Massachusetts*, III, 297.
[47] *Ibid.*
[48] Ford, "Social Conditions and Social Changes", *Commonwealth History of Massachusetts*, III, 508.

say, that although slavery is not smitten by an apoplexy, yet it has received a mortal wound, and will die of consumption.[49]

General William Heath directed his statements at those who felt the slave trade provisions of the Constitution were inadequate:

I apprehend that it is not in our power to do anything for or against those who are in slavery in the Southern States. No gentlemen within these walls detests every idea of slavery more than I do; it is generally destested by the people of the commonwealth; and I ardently hope the time will come when our brethren in the Southern States will view it as we do, and put a stop to it, but to this we have no right to compel them. Two questions naturally arise, if we ratify the constitution: Shall we do anything by our acts to hold the blacks in slavery? or shall we become partakers in other Men's sins? I think neither of them. Each state is sovereign and independent, to a certain degree; and they have a right to, and will regulate their own internal affairs as to themselves appears proper, and shall we refuse to eat, or to drink, or to be united with those who do not think or act just as we do? Truly not. We are not in this case partakers of other men's sins, for in nothing do we voluntarily encourage the slavery of our fellowmen.[50]

The spirit of these arguments shows, on the one hand, personal opposition to the enslavement of "our fellowmen" and a belief that the institution will eventually die out; on the other hand, it denies the right of interference by any body outside the state to regulate what the people of that state consider property. It further denies that failure of outsiders to interfere with slavery or willingness to associate with slaveholders impose a stigma of personal guilt.

It is quite obvious that the sentiments above largely duplicate the position held by John Adams in regard to the problem of Negro slavery. There is no evidence that Adams contributed directly to such thinking, and in only one instance, in 1777, did he display any concern for the stand his state took on the issue. Morally antagonistic to slavery on personal grounds, politically opposed to civil disorder, threats to national unity and property rights, Adams appears to have

---

[49] *Debate of the Convention of the Commonwealth of Massachusetts Convened at Boston on the 9th of January, 1788, and continued until the 7th of February for the Purpose of Assenting to and Ratifying the Constitution Recommended by the Grand Federal Convention* (Boston, Olive and Munroe and Joshem Cushing, 1808), 68. This may have been the William Dawes who accompanied Paul Revere on the famous midnight ride and at this date resided in Boston.
[50] *Ibid.*, 143-44.

reflected views on the question long held by the politically active majority in Massachusetts. Slavery came to the colony, was rejected by most and died a gentle death. During Adams' day the Negro as a slave touched the personal lives of few Massachusetts residents, and the attitude of minding one's own business appears to have prevailed. The free Negro roughneck who caused disturbances on the streets of Boston was another case. It was this Negro, rather than the slave, who at times aroused public concern which resulted in political action.

As for the some-time friends and political associates of John Adams, usually referred to as the Adams Federalists, there is no evidence that they deviated from the Massachusetts norm regarding the Negro problem. Free of any great anti-slavery pressure from home, it appears that they, like Adams, at times used the issue to promote their political interests. Considering the Federalist support forthcoming from large plantation owners during the Washington and Adams administrations, it is understandable, though hardly admirable, that neither Adams nor his followers would take a stand antagonistic to the slave interests. On the contrary, like Adams, some of them were not above appealing to the Southerner's concern for slavery in order to gain support for the party program. To win Southern acceptance for his anti-French policies, Pickering, in March of 1798, circulated a rumor via a letter to Robert G. Harper that France was secretly fomenting a slave insurrection in the South. Harrison Otis repeated the rumor in a pamphlet published in April of the same year.[51]

A few years later, when he and his fellows of the Essex Junto constituted the nucleus of the small band of extreme Federalists remaining in Congress, Pickering again appealed to Southern fears of slave insurrection. This time, however, there was little hope for support from the guardians of the "peculiar institution". The issue arose during the debate on the Louisiana Government Bill. The opposition of the Federalist extremists was limited to the clause which dealt with the existence of slavery in the territory. They expressed no desire to free the slaves already in Louisiana, but were determined to prevent the further growth of the institution. At this juncture Hillhouse of Connecticut and Pickering stressed the threat of slave revolt in an area where the blacks already outnumbered the whites.

[51] Stephen G. Kurtz, *The Presidency of John Adams* (Philadelphia, University of Pennsylvania Press, 1957), 313, citing Pickering MSS, Massachusetts Historical Society, X, 502, and Morison, *Otis*, I, 68, note 11.

Pickering offered to support an amendment which would make the importation of slaves into the territory a criminal act.[52] Obviously the purpose behind this supposed concern for the safety of white Louisianians was to prevent the further political growth of the slave interests, no longer their allies. A most significant aspect of this incident is that the New Englanders obviously were not yet disposed to level their attack directly upon slavery.

John Quincy Adams, sitting in the Senate during the debates on the Louisiana Bill, gave no indication that he would one day lead the anti-slavery forces in Congress. Like his father and other Massachusetts representatives before him, he was not bound by his constituents to take a stand on slavery, and following tradition he separated personal convictions from political action on the question. Therefore he voted against all amendments limiting the slave trade in Louisiana, including one which prohibited the importation of any slave except by a citizen of the United States going to the territory for actual settlement. The latter measure passed the Senate by a vote of twenty-one to seven. His nominal reason for the vote was that, though opposed to slavery, he was equally opposed to Congress legislating for the territory and also felt that Congress was "proceeding with too much haste upon such an important question".[53] Earlier he had made a remark which provides a perfect example of his ability to separate personal views on slavery from more practical concerns of the day. "Slavery in a moral sense is an evil, but as connected with commerce it has its uses." [54]

At this stage of his career the younger Adams took no opportunity to speak out unequivocally against either the slave trade or the expansion of slavery. His principal grievance against slavery during these Senatorial years was the article in the Constitution which allowed five slaves to be counted as three whites in apportioning representatives in the House of Representatives.[55] His father had also found fault with the preferential treatment accorded Southerners,

[52]   Harvey Putnum Prentiss, *Timothy Pickering as the Leader of New England Federalism, 1800-1815* (Evanston, Illinois, Northwestern University, 1932), 22, citing William Plumer, *Memorandum of Proceedings in Senate,* 1803-07, memo 121.

[53]   Samuel Flagg Bemis, *John Quincy Adams and the Foundations of American Foreign Policy* (New York, Alfred A. Knopf, 1949), 122, citing J. Q. Adams, *Memoirs,* I, 346.

[54]   *Ibid.,* citing Plumer, *Memoirs of Proceedings in Senate,* 1803-07, 413.

[55]   *Ibid.,* 122-23.

when he spoke out against excluding slaves from the total population to be taxed.

John Quincy Adams' career in the diplomatic arena as an American minister abroad and Secretary of State at home brought him into public contact with international problems arising out of the existence of slavery. Like his father before him, he did not let personal views regarding the "peculiar institution" of his country interfere with his official responsibilities. He loyally presented the claims of Southern owners for indemnification for their slaves abducted by the British forces after the Peace of Ghent; he lent the assistance of the Department of State to Southern attempts to extradite escaped slaves from Canada; he showed no sympathy for the American Colonization Society and advised the President that its aims would lead to imperialism.[56]

Though John Quincy Adams' convictions regarding slavery and politics began to undergo a change during the Missouri crises, he remained silent. His Transcontinental Treaty could not be passed by antagonizing the South, and besides, the anti-slavery cause was as yet by no means a popular movement to which he could look for support. During the campaigns of 1824 and 1828 and during his tenure as President, he remained silent on the issue.[57]

In 1831 John Quincy Adams entered the House of Representatives to begin the second phase of his public career. His association with John C. Calhoun and the result of the election of 1828 had convinced him that the South was determined to uphold the cause of free and unlimited expansion of slavery, even at the cost of dissolving the Union.[58] In his first address in the House, Adams read petitions against the slave trade in the District of Columbia, but at the same time he put himself on record as not agreeing with the prayers for abolition in the nation's capital.[59]

John Quincy Adams' fight was for the liberty of petition and the prevention of the expansion of slavery. These stands he could take with the assurance of growing support in his home state. But as his father's son and a representative of responsible Massachusetts opinion, he could not aline himself with the abolition forces. As late as August

[56]   Ibid., 416, citing J. Q. Adams, Memoirs, IV, 292.
[57]   Samuel Flagg Bemis, John Quincy Adams and the Union (New York, Alfred A. Knopf, 1956), 26, 64, 147, 328.
[58]   Ibid., 150.
[59]   Ibid., 331, citing J. Q. Adams, Memoirs, VIII, 434 (December 12, 1831).

21, 1835, the "best citizens" of Boston met at Faneuil Hall to denounce the Anti-Slavery Society. Men like Peley Sprague, Richard Fletcher, Theodore Lyman, Jr., Harrison Gray Otis, and Edward Everett demanded laws to curb the activities of the abolitionist fanatics.[60]

The approach to the Negro problem taken by John Adams was followed in many respects by his son. Their stated positions on issues regarding the Negro were to a great extent influenced and guided by the views of the public they served. That indices of works dealing with John Quincy Adams contain numerous references to the Negro whereas those dealing with his father are often void of the subject can probably be attributed in large measure to the fact that, during at least part of the lifetime of the former, personal convictions regarding slavery corresponded to some degree with political expediency.

[60] Oswald Garrison Villard, "The Antislavery Crises in Massachusetts, 1830-1850", *Commonwealth History of Massachusetts*, IV, 312.

CHAPTER II

JOHN ADAMS AND THE INDIAN

In 1812 John Adams wrote Thomas Jefferson a lengthy letter in which the Indian was the chief topic of discussion. He told Jefferson of a life-long "interest in the Indians and a commisseration for them" and recalled the experiences of his boyhood when dignitaries of nearby tribes and members of an Indian family, whose "wigwam" was but a mile away, were frequent visitors at the Adams home. There were also the times remembered when "I ... used to call at their wigwam, where I never failed to be treated with worthelberries, blackberries. ..." But the seventy-seven year old Adams also had other memories. "I remember the time when Indian murders, scalpings, depredations, and conflagrations were as frequent on the eastern and northern frontiers of Massachusetts as they are now in Indiana, and spread as much terror." [1]

Surprisingly, neither the expressed interest in and concern for the Indians' welfare nor the romantic recollections of a boyhood among red men are reflected in the early writings of Adams. Prior to the Revolution there is but a single diary reference to Indians, and this is merely a comment about the duration of the "bloody" war with the Cherokees and French in 1760.[2] After 1774, though not frequent, the references to the Indian are more numerous. From this point the degree and nature of his interest in the Indian appears to have been largely influenced by the circumstances in which he found himself as well as the activities of the tribes.

During the Revolutionary War years the scattered references to the red men appearing in Adams' writings are concerned with the Indians as military allies or enemies in the struggle with Britain. While there are no expressions of commiseration, there is evidence of a certain fascination which perhaps mirrored the conflicting im-

[1] C. F. Adams, *Works*, X, 19-20 (June 28, 1812).
[2] Butterfield, *Diary and Autobiography*, I, 185 (December 27, 1760).

pressions of his youth — those tales of Indian terror on the frontier and the contrastingly delightful experiences with his Indian neighbors in Braintree. In discussing with James Warren the possible employment of Indian warriors by the British it is likely that Adams called to mind the more frightening memories of his boyhood:

The Indians are known to conduct their Wars so entirely without Faith and Humanity that it will bring eternal Infamy on the Ministry throughout all Europe if they should excite those Savages to War. . . . To let loose those blood Hounds to scalp Men and to butcher Women and Children is horrid.[3]

In 1776 Adams expressed to Warren his concern that the British might use Canada as a base for Indian operations "and perhaps enduce them to take up the Hatchet and commit their Robberies and Murders upon the Frontier".[4]

When Adams had an opportunity to come face to face with friendly Indians during these same years, his reaction was quite different. A mixture of curiosity, delight, and admiration replaced the grim vision of scalping and butchery. On January 24, 1776, Adams wrote in his diary of a dinner in Cambridge in the distinguished company of Generals Washington and Gates and their wives. However, the great attraction of the evening for Adams was obviously the presence of "half a dozen sachems and warriors of the French Caghnawaga tribe, with their wives and children . . .". The Adams who penned his impressions of that evening displayed all the enthusiasm of a youngster just returned from his first visit to the circus. "It was a savage feast, carnivorous animals devouring their prey, yet they were wondrous polite. The General introduced me to them as one of the grand council fire at Philadelphia, upon which they made me as many bows and a cordial reception." [5]

In his autobiography Adams recalled his first appearance at the Court of Versailles in June, 1778, and at the same time provided us with another example of his reaction to contacts with friendly Indians:

I [found] myself gazed at, as We in America used to gaze at the Indians who came to make Speeches to Us in Congress, but I thought it very hard if I could not command as much Power of face, as one of the Chiefs of the

---

[3] *Warren-Adams Letters*, I, 53 (June 7, 1775).
[4] *Ibid.*, I, 208 (February 18, 1776).
[5] Butterfield, *Diary and Autobiography*, II, 226-27. Adams also described the events at Mifflin's in a letter to his wife. Butterfield, *Family Correspondence*, I, 343 (January 24, 1776).

Six Nations, and therefore determined that I would assume a chearful countenance, enjoy the Scene around me and observe it cooly as an astronomer contemplates the Stars.[6]

During the years following the Revolution and prior to his elevation to the Presidency Adams' references to the Indian primarily dealt with their customs, traditions and institutions. At The Hague in 1782 he answered several inquiries about Indian customs. Unfortunately, his diary provides neither the questions nor his responses to them.[7] Adams devoted part of his time as minister to the Court of Saint James to writing *A Defense of the Constitution of the Government of the United States of America.* In this work he called upon his concept of Indian tribal government to prove "that 3 branches of power have an unalterable foundation in nature; that they exist in every society, natural and artificial...."[8] Adams wrote:

Every nation in North America has a king, senate, and a people. The royal office is elective, but it is for life; his sachems are his ordinary council, where all the national affairs are deliberated and resolved in the first instance; but in the greatest of all, which is declaring war, the king and sachems call a national assembly round a great council fire, communicate to the people their resolution, and sacrifice an animal.[9]

During Adams' eight years as Vice President, an office he regarded as "the most insignificant ... that ever invention of man contrived, or his imagination conceived", the Indian presented one of the most serious problems facing the young nation.[10] To pacify the tribes extensive military campaign were undertaken, culminating in Anthony Wayne's victory at Fallen Timbers. Diplomatic negotiations which led to the Jay and Pinckney Treaties were closely allied to the Indian problem. In 1796 Congress established trading factories in the hope of ensuring continued peace.[11]

[6]   *Ibid.,* IV, 133.
[7]   *Ibid.,* III, 5. In a diary entry dated September 14, 1782 (Holland), Adams wrote, "The General [Vander Dussen] was inquisitive after the American Savages and a great Part of our Conservation consisted in his Questions and my Answers concerning them."
[8]   C. F. Adams, *Works,* IV, 579 (1787).
[9]   *Ibid.,* IV, 566.
[10]   Adams' statement regarding the Vice Presidency was made in a letter to his wife; Charles Francis Adams (ed.), *Letters of John Adams Addressed to His Wife* (Boston, C. C. Little and J. Brown, 1841), II, 133 (December 19, 1793).
[11]   George D. Harmon, *Sixty Years of Indian Affairs; Political, Economic, and*

Through all this Adams appears to have remained silent. His writings show no concern for either the terrorized white settlers or the defeated Indians. There is no evidence that he offered advice either on military matters or on methods of establishing permanent peace on the frontiers. In fact, the only notable reference to the Indian among his published writings of this period is contained in *Davila*, where the Indian is employed to illustrate that nations "civilized and uncivilized, have their beloved families...".[12]

Adams' election to the Presidency seems to have brought him back to the world of day-to-day reality were the Indian was concerned. His inaugural address was precedent breaking in many respects. It was the first time he spoke in public on the Indian problem; it was apparently the first time since the Revolution that he made a comment of any kind regarding contemporary Indian affairs, and it was the first evidence of an expressed concern for the sufferings of the Indians. Despite all this, however, what he said was brief and certainly non-commital. Without defining the problem or offering a concrete program, he called for "a spirit of equality and humanity toward the aboriginal nations of America, and a disposition to meliorate their condition by inclining them to be more friendly to us and our citizens to be more friendly to them...."[13]

The brevity and vagueness of this passage in reality foreshadowed the President's Indian policy. His administration was the beneficiary of the military and diplomatic successes of the Washington years. When Adams took office in 1797, the frontier was relatively quiet. The various pronouncements which he issued regarding Indian policy — all limited to his first two years in office — appear not to have been directed toward a permanent solution of any kind, but rather to the maintenance of the favorable status quo.

Adams first turned his attention to the unfinished business inherited from his predecessor. The terms of Jay's Treaty of San Lorenzo had yet to be completely fulfilled. For one thing, the Spanish had not abandoned all their posts north of the thirty-first parallel. Adams' concern over this situation was expressed to Congress on November 23, 1797. "These circumstances are the more to be regretted, as they

---

Diplomatic, 1789-1850 (Chapel Hill, N.C., The University of North Carolina Press, 1941), 100-01.

[12] C. F. Adams, *Works*, VI, 299.

[13] *Ibid.*, IX, 109 (March 4, 1797).

cannot fail to affect the Indians in a manner injurious to the United States." [14]

Just as fears of Indian hostilities had prompted Adams' insistence that one aspect of the treaty be fulfilled, this same concern led him to take a different position on another clause of the same treaty. On December 8, 1798, Adams told Congress:

Recent information renders it probable that the southern Indians, either instigated to oppose the demarkation, or jealous of the consequences of suffering white people to run a line over lands to which the Indian title had not been extinguished, have ere this time stopped the progress of the commissioners, and considering the mishaps which may result from continuing the demarkation, in opposition to the will of the Indian tribes, the great expense attending it, and that the boundaries, which the commission have actually established, probably extend at least as far as the Indian title has been extinguished, it will perhaps become expedient and necessary to suspend further proceeding by recalling our commissioners.[15]

During the period 1797 to 1801, only one Indian treaty was presented to the Senate which could be traced to the initiative of the Adams administration. On January 8, 1798, Adams told the Senate, "The situation of affairs between some of the citizens of the United States and the Cherokee Indians has evinced the propriety of holding a treaty with that nation to extinguish by purchase their right to certain parcels of land and to adjust and settle other points relative to the safety and conveniency of our citizens." [16] Nine days later he told both Houses that the intention of this treaty was "the promotion of justice to them [Indians], as well as the interests and convenience of our citizens".[17] On October 2, 1798, Adams submitted the Cherokee Treaty of Tellica for ratification without further comment.[18]

On April 12, 1798, Adams presented a treaty with the Mohawk Nation to the Senate. This treaty had been negotiated by the previous administration and had "by accident lain long neglected".[19] On May 3, 1798, upon the request of Governor John Jay of New York, he appointed a commission to treat with the Oneida tribe.[20] In neither

14 *Ibid.*, 123.
15 *Ibid.*, 132.
16 James D. Richardson (ed.), *A Compilation of the Messages and Papers of the Presidents, 1797-1897* (Washington, Published by Authority of Congress, 1898), I, 259.
17 *Ibid.*, 260.
18 *Ibid.*, 281.
19 *Ibid.*, 265.
20 *Ibid.*, 266.

of these instances did the President offer opinions of any sort.

In a letter written to James Lloyd after he left the White House, John Adams expressed pride and complete satisfaction with his handling of Indian affairs while President:

I was engaged in the most earnest, sedulous, and I must own, expensive' exertion to preserve peace with the Indians, and prepare them for agriculture and civilization, through the whole of my administration. I had the inexpressible satisfaction of complete success. Not a hatchet was lifted in my time; and the single battle of Tippecanoe has since cost the United States a hundred times more money than it cost me to maintain universal and perpetual peace. . . . My labors were indefatigable to compose all difficulties and settle all controversies with all nations, civilized and savage.[21]

The fact that "not a hatchet was lifted" during the period of his administration would provide pleasant memories for any former President. However, the personal credit taken by Adams for this phenomenon appears largely unwarranted. Faced with a rather stable Indian situation upon taking office, Adams merely took steps to check any immediate threats to peace. He neither spoke of nor initiated long range programs to prevent future clashes between whites and Indians, and there is no evidence to confirm his claims regarding efforts to "prepare them for agriculture and civilization". The provisions of the 1796 act establishing trading factories ran out after two years and no action was taken by the administration to urge renewal. When Adams left the Presidency, only two government factories were in existence, maintaining themselves on the original appropriation of funds.[22]

The reference to civilizing the Indians reflected the desires of many men of Adams' day. However, Adams himself does not seem to have been deeply concerned with that possibility. He refused to accept those optimistic, romantic concepts of Indian life and thought from which proponents of a program for civilizing the red men drew much of their faith and strength. He wrote to Benjamin Waterhouse, "I am not . . . of Rousseau's Opinion. His notions of the purest morals in savage Nations and the earliest Ages of civilized Nations are mere Chimeras." [23] In the margin of his copy of Rousseau's Discourse on

[21] C. F. Adams, Works, X, 153 (March 31, 1815).
[22] Harmon, Sixty Years of Indian Affairs, 108.
[23] Worthington Chauncey Ford (ed.), Statesman and Friend, Correspondence of John Adams with Benjamin Waterhouse, 1784-1822 (Boston, Little, Brown, and Co., 1927), 123 (Feb. 26, 1817).

Inequality, he had written, "Reasonings from a State of Nature are fallacious because hypothetical. We have no facts. Experiments are wanting. Reasoning from Savage Life do not much better. Every writer affirms what he pleases. We have not facts to depend on." [24] Adams also had little support to offer those who compared the metaphysical concepts of the Indians with those of the Jews or Greeks. "The Indians were not metaphysicians enough to have discovered this idea, the intermediate power between good and evil, God and matter. But of the two powers, the good and the evil, they seem to have a conviction; and what son or daughter of Adam and Eve has not?" [25] As for theories of Indian origin, which held a fascination for so many of his contemporaries, Adams wrote:

I would as soon suppose that the Prodigal Son, in a frolic with one of his Girls made a trip to America in one of Mother Carey's Eggshells, and left the fruit of their Amours: as believe any of the grave hypotheses and solemn reasonings of the Philosophers or Devines upon the Subject of the peopoling of America. If my faith in Moses or Noah depended on any of these speculations, I would give it up. [26]

It is probable that Adams' curiosity regarding the Indians and their institutions occupied a rather secondary position among his spheres of interest. Thoughts about the Indian seem to have arisen only when Adams called on his knowledge of them to illustrate some larger philosophical concept or when stimulated by some particular event in which Indians were involved. Just as the Revolutionary War and his duties as President caused Adams to focus attention on the Indian problem, the warfare centering around our second conflict with Great Britain reawakened an interest that had apparently been dormant for many years.

On May 2, 1812, Adams initiated a series of letters to Thomas Jefferson in which he asked the Sage of Monticello various questions regarding the Indian. Adams himself provides the clue for his renewed attention to the subject. "I know not what, unless it were the prophet of Tippecanoe, had turned my curiosity to inquiries after the meta-

[24] Roy Harvey Pearce, *The Savages of America* (Baltimore, The Johns Hopkins Press, 1953), 106, citing "John Adams on Rousseau", *More Books,* I (Bulletin of the Boston Public Library, 1926).
[25] C. F. Adams, *Works,* X, 18-19. To Thomas Jefferson (June 28, 1812).
[26] L. J. Cappon, *Adams-Jefferson Letters,* II, 328, To Thomas Jefferson (June 11, 1813).

physical science of the Indians, their ecclesiastical establishments and their theological theories. . . ." [27]

In the ensuing correspondence Adams revealed his attitude toward the various theories of Indian origin and concepts of Indian metaphysical thought and told of his youthful associations with Indians around Braintree and his long interest and concern for this race, all of which have been referred to earlier in this chapter. The letters also provide an understanding of just how thorough Adams' knowledge of the Indian was. At one point Adams thanked Jefferson for a list of books concerning the Indian and stated, "It has given me satisfaction because, while it has furnished me with information where all the knowledge is to be obtained that books afford, it has convinced me that I shall never know much more of the subject than I do now. As I have never aimed at making any collection of books upon this subject, and have none of those you abridged in so concise a manner." At another point Adams admitted to having previously been in error regarding Indian religious practices. He stated that his belief in the existence of an order of priests in tribal society had been based upon childhood impressions of the local Indians.[28]

Though stimulated by Tecumseh and the War of 1812, the direction of Adams' renewed interest in the Indian was far removed from the grave problems which faced white and red men in this critical period. Only once in his exchanges with Jefferson did he refer to the current warfare. In his lengthy letter of June 28, 1812, he expressed his belief that another conquest of Canada would "quiet the Indian forever and be as great a blessing to them as to us." [29]

How limited Adams' interest in the Indian problem appears to have been! How shortsighted was his approach to the solution of the complex dilemma! Adams' confidence that a conquest of Canada would put an end to Indian warfare was voiced during the Revolution as well as in 1812.[30] This short-term approach of removing what he felt was the immediate stimulant to Indian dissatisfaction was reflected in the few steps he took as President.

One of Adams' last references to the Indian is contained in a letter dated September 23, 1818. In it Adams, at the age of eighty-three, set forth an opinion apparently for the first and last time on the basic

[27]   C. F. Adams, *Works*, X, 17 (June 28, 1812).
[28]   *Ibid.*, 17, 20 (June 28, 1812).
[29]   *Ibid.*, 20.
[30]   *Warren-Adams Letters*, I, 208, To Joseph Warren (February 18, 1776).

issue of the Indian problem, i. e. white man's desire to expand into, settle, and cultivate land held by the Indian and the latter's equally strong desire to maintain his domain and to continue to utilize it for hunting and fishing. As might be expected, Adams arrived at this discussion rather indirectly. The basic question at hand was the Colonies' right to revolt against England and in doing so deprive the mother country of its legally owned territory. Adams' answer was that the right of ownership lies in the hands who occupy and utilize the land to its fullest capacity. The Indian was brought in to illustrate his point:

Shall we say that a few handful of scattering tribes of savages have a right of domain and property of a quarter of this globe capable of nourishing hundreds of millions of happy human beings? Why had not Europeans a right to come and hunt and fish with them?

The Indian has a right to life, liberty, and property in common with all men; but what right to domain or property beyond these? Every Indian has a right to his wigwam, his armor, his utensils; when he had burned the woods about him, and planted his corn and beans, his squashes and pompions, all these were his undoubtful right; but will you infer from this, that he had rights of exclusive dominion and property of immense regions of uncultivated wilderness that he never saw, that he might have the exclusive privilege of hunting and fishing in them, which he himself never expected or hoped to enjoy?[31]

Adams continued on to describe past relations with the American Indians. He expressed his opinion that the white men had been just in their treatment of the tribes, had respected rights to property which the Indians actually possessed and obtained such lands only by legal treaties. "There is scarcely a litigation at law concerning a title to land that may not be traced to an Indian deed ... and this was the general practice through the continent." Adams summed up his history of Indian relations with the following statement: "In short, I see not how the Indians could have been treated with more equity or humanity than they have been in general in North America."[32]

What about the numerous and bloody wars which did so much to thin the Indian ranks? Were not these caused by what the Indians at least considered unfair pressure to surrender their lands? Adams provided an answer. "The histories of Indian wars have not been sufficiently regarded." He insisted that all attempts to introduce

[31] C. F. Adams, *Works*, X, 354-60, To William Tudor (September 29, 1818).
[32] *Ibid.*, 360.

agriculture, to provide education and to convert "these poor, ignorant savages" to Christianity had failed because of the tenacity to which the Indian held to his religion and concluded, "It is a principle of religion, at bottom, which inspires the Indians with such an invincible aversion both to civilization and Christianity. The same principle has excited their perpetual hostilities against the colonies and independent Americans." [33]

This picture which Adams painted for his former law apprentice, Judge William Tudor, was a study in black and white. It portrayed the white man as just, considerate and striving to better the conditions of the Indian. It showed the Indian as a negative and hostile captive of his religion. Thus, Adams, who just a few years earlier displayed a misunderstanding of Indian theology in his admittedly mistaken concept of the existence of an order of priests, presented an interpretation of the Indian problem in which religion was of primary importance.

If one accepts the belief that the Indian's religion was at the root of his misfortune, it would appear logical to surmise that the best road to salvation, spiritual and temporal, would be conversion to another religion, which in the majority of white American minds implies conversion to Christianity. This missionary doctrine was not new in Adams' day. The choice of sword and damnation or Christianity and salvation had been offered before to the heathens. The Moors of Spain, for one, had experienced the missionary zeal of the conquering Christians and, as will be illustrated later in this chapter, so too had the Indians of colonial Massachusetts. It is possible that this doctrine governed Adams' thinking relative to the Indian problem. Perhaps he felt that as President he could accomplish little in the way of introducing civilization to the Indians until the forces of religion accomplished their work.

However, the problem in reaching such an assumption concerning Adams lies in the fact that one can in no way be certain how accurately the opinions expressed in this letter represented Adams' thinking during his politically active years or, for that matter, even at the age of eighty-three. There is no evidence of his ever before having expressed such views, and it must be remembered that in the letter he was taking a defensive position. His primary purpose was to defend the American Revolution as a legal act. Adams did this by drawing an analogy to what he must have considered any intelligent

[33] *Ibid.*, 361-62.

individual would view as the logical and legal right of the civilized man to usurp the domain of the savage. Thus, one is led to suspect that the opinions stated in this letter relative to the Indian were probably drawn largely from prevailing notions rather than from strongly held personal convictions and done so primarily for the purpose of serving his analogy.

It is interesting to note that in 1815, three years prior to the letter to Judge Tudor, Adams had proclaimed proudly that during his administration his "exertions" to prepare the Indians for agriculture and civilization had met with "complete success".[34] Since there is no evidence of any such "exertions" on his part, and since his claim to "complete success" is contrary to the facts of history and to his comment to Tudor of "how little success" had been achieved in these endeavors, one is forced to conclude that Adams here engaged in a bit of exaggeration in defense of his Presidential leadership.

The combination of Adams' mild interest in Indian life, apparent misconceptions about some of their customs and practices and lack of real concern with the Indian problem can probably be explained in part by his Massachusetts background. Adams was born early enough to have had some contact with Indians in his boyhood years. His ears must have been filled with tales of Indian warfare. As late as 1697 Braintree had been subject to a small incursion by French and Indians, and earlier, Braintree men had participated in King Philip's War.[35] But the experiences of Adams' youth, while creating the basis for a curiosity about the Indian, could hardly have provided an education useful in approaching the Indian problems of early national America. The relationship between the handful of Ponkhapoags who lived in Adams' Braintree and the Indian warriors who roamed the forests of the frontier must have been quite remote. By 1735, the year of Adams' birth, the Indians of Massachusetts were well on their way to virtual extinction. Disease had struck the savages a devastating blow even before the Pilgrims landed at Cape Cod. Johnson's *Wonder Working Providence* relates that the most "admirable Act of Christ preparing for his people's arrival in the Western World [was] consumption, sweeping away whole Families, but chiefly young Men and Children, the very seeds of increase [so that] their wigwams lie full of dead corpses — by this means Christ not

[34]   *Ibid.*, 153, To James Lloyd (March 31, 1815).
[35]   William S. Pattee, *A History of Old Braintree and Quincy* (Quincy, Green and Prescott, 1878), 366, 549.

only made room for his people to plant, but also tamed the hard and cruel hearts of those barbarous Indians." [36]

With the conclusion of King Philip's War in 1678 the Indian threat in Massachusetts was all but eliminated. The warring tribes had been nearly wiped out, and many of the survivors fled westward into New York.[37] The concerns of the General Court in the eighteenth century reflect the fact that the Indian problem by Adams' day had become largely a matter of police work. As was pointed out in the previous chapter, the various laws which were concerned with preventing public disturbances tended to lump the Indian with the Negro and mulatto.

It is doubtful that more than a handful of Indians were even affected by such laws. Their numbers were minute by the time Adams established residency in Boston. The census of 1790 listed 800 Indians in Massachusetts, all located in the vicinity of Cape Cod, Martha's Vineyard and Bristol County. It is therefore unlikely that the Indians represented a noticeable percentage of the 761 colored people attributed to Boston in 1790.[38]

Official Massachusetts did little to encourage the Indian to adopt white man's civilization and take his place as a first-class citizen. Indian slavery was officially recognized, though it gradually died out in the eighteenth century. By the end of the seventeenth century Indians were in such short supply that they were imported primarily, from the Carolinas, for the purpose of providing slaves.[39] In 1712 the General Court prohibited further imports of that nature and thus contributed to eventual extinction of Indian slavery. However, the stated reasons for the Act were far from humane. It was pointed out that the Indian slaves imported from the South were "malicious, surly and revengeful", that the industry of the colony was unlike that of the West Indies, that with savage enemies at hand it was danger-ous to have bondsmen of a kindred race, and that the influx of slaves discouraged the importation of Christian servants.[40]

The task of Christianizing the Indians was largely left to individual

[36] Cited in F. J. Stimson, "Massachusetts in Literature, The 17th Century", *Commonwealth History of Massachusetts*, I, 371.
[37] John Gould Curtis, "Expansion and King Philip's War", *Commonwealth History of Massachusetts*, I, 553.
[38] Bureau of the Census, *A Century of Population Growth*, 39, 84. Indians were also listed in the "colored" category in the census.
[39] Allyn Barley Forbes, "Social Life in Town and Country", *Commonwealth History of Massachusetts*, II, 264.
[40] Almon Wheeler Lauber, *Indian Slavery in Colonial Times Within the Present*

preachers and missionary societies, though in the seventeenth century
the government did show some concern for this work. In 1644 the
General Court ordered the shire courts to assume the responsibility
for civilizing the Indians and supervising their religious instruction.⁴¹
In 1646, after having sought advice from the clergy the previous year,
the General Court ordered ministers to elect two of their number
to preach the gospel to the Indians.⁴² In 1677 it was decreed that all
the Indian captives taken in King Philip's war be distributed as slaves
amongst the colonists and "be taught and instructed in the Christian
religion".⁴³ Adams need not have looked beyond the borders of his
own state for an excellent example of the failure of the Indians to
embrace Christianity. Through the efforts of John Eliot and other
missionaries an estimated four thousand savages had been converted
to the status of Praying Indians by the eve of King Philip's War.⁴⁴
However, a list drawn up in 1698 gave only twenty-five hundred as
the number of converts in the Indian towns and pointed out that
most of these were dying off rapidly.⁴⁵

The Massachusetts example provides evidence to show that more
than the tenacity with which the Indian held to his religion was
involved in his downfall. To put it simply, the Massachusetts divines
viewed the Indians as tools of Satan, employed by him to prevent
the occupation of that land chosen by God for his people. Two
weapons could be employed against such an obstacle, conversion and
war. The latter with its ally, disease, was by far the most effective
in Masachusetts.

The governments of Massachusetts initiated and condoned policies
which could have led to no other end but the destruction of the
Indians. They sanctioned Indian slavery. In 1636 they eliminated
the Pequot power by initiating a war on largely trumped-up charges.
A generation later they struck down their former allies in the cruel

---

Limits of the United States (New York, Columbia University, 1913), 188, citing
Acts and Resolves, I, 698 (August 23, 1712).
⁴¹ William Kellaway, *The New England Company, 1649-1776* (New York,
Barnes and Noble, Inc., 1961), 11, citing N. B. Shurtleff (ed.), *Records of the
Governor and Company of the Massachusetts Bay* (Boston, 1853), III, 96-97.
⁴² Pearce, *The Savages of America,* 27.
⁴³ Lauber, *Indian Slavery,* 273, citing Shurtleff, *Records of the Governor and
Company of the Massachusetts Bay,* V, 136.
⁴⁴ Curtis, "Expansion and King Philip's War", *Commonwealth History of
Massachusetts,* I, 539.
⁴⁵ Pearce, *The Savages of America,* 29-30, citing Noyes, *New England Duty
and Interest,* appendix.

King Philip's War. In all their wars with the Indians the Puritans distinguished themselves by wholesale massacres of non-combatants and the selling into slavery of the survivors. The support given these activities by the Puritan divines was considerable. They repeatedly employed Biblical interpretations to prove that it was the sacred duty of the Christians to root out the godless Canaanites.[46]

It is difficult to determine exactly how and to what extent Adams' view of the Indian problem was influenced by his Massachusetts background. His hesitancy to initiate a strong Indian policy appears to have more nearly reflected his contemporary home environment with its virtual absence of an Indian problem than the example of his Puritan forebears. However, in the letter to William Tudor in which Adams defended the right of the civilized white to expand into Indian territory and placed the blame for the Indians' misfortune on their religion, there can be observed an echo of his forefathers' reasoning. There is some resemblance to the Old Testament analogy of the right of the Children of Israel to invade Canaan and occupy the land of the heathens. The early Puritans also recognized the principle that ownership of land is related to utilization of the soil. John Winthrop had written in 1629:

. . . the whole earth is the Lord's garden and he hath given it to the sons of Adam to be tilled and improved by them. Why then should we stand starving here for the places of habitation, (many men spending as much labor and cost to recover or keep sometimes an acre or two of lands as would procure him many hundreds of acres, as good or better, in another place) and in the meantime suffer whole countries, as profitable for the use of man, to be wasted without any improvement.[47]

It is not unlikely that the Puritan in Adams was also a factor in his rejection of the romantic concepts of the savage, just as it strengthened his conviction that they were all sons and daughters of Adam and Eve.

The Massachusetts environment, which did so little to arouse in Adams an interest in or understanding of the contemporary Indian problem, appears to have had a similar effect on Adams' fellow Massachusetts politicians. There is no evidence of their displaying

[46] Alvin M. Josephy, Jr., *American Heritage Book of Indians* (Washington, D.C., American Heritage Publishing Co., Inc., 1961), 171-74. Also, Pearce, *Savages of America*, 23-24.

[47] Pearce, *Savages of America*, 21, citing Winthrop's "General Considerations", in Young's *Chronicles of the First Planters*, 272.

any interest whatsoever in the Indian problem. Lacking the scholarly, inquiring mind of Adam, they appear to have virtually ignored the Indian's existence.

John Quincy Adams, like his father, displayed no long time concern with the Indian problem. Though as diplomat, cabinet member and President he faced the issue more often than had the elder Adams, John Quincy's approach was none the less similar to his father's in many respects. At one point in his early career the younger Adams looked back on the history of relations between the races and expressed views quite similar to those found in his father's letter to Tudor. In 1802 he delivered a Plymouth Rock Oration in which he extolled the heroic virtues of the Pilgrim Fathers and strongly supported their right and that of all Europeans to form settlements in the American wilderness and establish sovereignty over the aborigines.[48] During the negotitions leading to the Treaty of Ghent he offered a similar argument, defending the Indian policy of the United States. He declared that it was the moral and religious duty of a civilized nation to settle, cultivate, and improve the Indian territory, extinguishing step by step the right of savage tribes by fair and amicable means — a principle, said he, perfectly recognized by the law of nations.[49] By the end of his career, however, John Quincy Adams had come to a quite different view of the situation. In 1837 he wrote, "We have done more harm to the Indian since our Revolution than had ever been done to them by the French and English nations before. . . . These are crying sins for which we are answerable before a higher jurisdiction. . . ."[50]

The sentiments expressed in John Quincy Adams' messages to Congress were similar to those of his father's inaugural. He added the hope, popular in his day, that transplanting the Indians west of the Mississippi would lead to civilization and eventual citizenship, but he did not pursue such a plan nor initiate a new or strong Indian policy of any kind. He listened to and supported in principle the hopeful proposals of his Secretary of War, Barbour, who envisioned a day when the Indians would establish territorial governments west of the Mississippi and eventually be amalgamated with the whites. However, in the private confines of his diary Adams had to accept

[48]   Cited in Bemis, *J. Q. A. Foundations*, 113.
[49]   *Ibid.*, 207-08, citing *American State Papers, Foreign Relations*, III, 719-21.
[50]   Bemis, *J. Q. A. and the Union*, 87, citing Adams, MSS., To S. S. Gregory (November 23, 1837).

the view of Clay as more nearly approaching reality. "I fear there is no practicable plan by which they can be organized into one civilized or half-civilized government." [51] In his message to Congress in 1828, John Quincy Adams reviewed the history of the government's Indian policy from the establishment of the Constitution. There was no trace of the pessimism found in his diary or the strong criticism set forth less than a decade later. "As independent powers we negotiated with them by treaties; as proprietors, we purchased of them all the land we could prevail to sell; as brethern of the human race, rude and ignorant, we endeavored to bring them to the knowledge of religion and of letters." [52]

Both father and son, while declaring the right of civilized man to eventual control over the domain of the savage, acted in such a way as to bring no dishonor to their New England consciences. John Quincy's dispute with Georgia's Governor Troup over the Cherokee lands could be held up as evidence of justice toward the Indians just as could his father's halting of the running of the boundary line. Both men gave lip service to a desire to civilize and Christianize the Indian. However, neither would publicly admit the possibility of extinction of the race, accept the premise that the white man in general was guilty of inhumane treatment of the Indian, or attempt to initiate policies which would alter the course of events.

The Indian, like the Negro, aroused in John Adams a degree of interest and a measure of sympathy, but Massachusetts was even further from the Indian villages of the frontier than the slave plantations of the South. Adams appears to have viewed the color problem as a flea on the body politic. It warranted attention only when it affected the interests of the state, nation and property rights. Sometimes, cupped in his palm, he used it to gain attention, but more often he brushed it aside.

---

[51] *Ibid.*, 84-85, citing J. Q. A., *Memoirs*, VII, 113.
[52] Richardson, *Messages*, II, 415-16 (December 2, 1828).

CHAPTER III

THOMAS JEFFERSON AND THE NEGRO

Throughout the years historians have recorded the names of men who have performed great deeds of service for their nation. Thomas Jefferson ranks high among these outstanding figures. When compared with all but a few, he seems unique. For he was one of those rare personages whose name has been employed as an adjective to describe a concept of government, an approach to science and education, a way of thinking, an entire era. His deeds helped to establish a nation. His thoughts have influenced men to the present day. Individuals representing all shades of the political spectrum have called upon his name to support their particular brands of democracy and their positions on great issues. The phenomenon of having exponents of all sides of a question claim Jefferson's support is a tribute to the great man's prestige, but, to say the least, it causes considerable confusion among the uncommitted and those seeking the truth.[1]

The color problem is an example of this. Racists and integrationists, abolitionists, and states righters have claimed Jefferson as their own. This chapter and the one which follows will attempt to reveal Jefferson's position on the color problem through an investigation of his writings and thus present a clearer view of the man and the era in which he lived and whose destiny he did so much to shape.

Unlike John Adams, Jefferson was immediately and personally involved in the slavery problem. In 1774 his wife's inheritance added one hundred and thirty-five slaves to his own collection of fifty.[2] The memoirs of his slave Isaac tell us that Jefferson was a "mighty good master" who offered encouragement and rewards for work well

---

[1] A great part of Merrill R. Peterson's work, *The Jefferson Image in the American Mind* (New York, Oxford University Press, 1960), 548 pp., is devoted to a discussion of this phenomenon.
[2] Dumas Malone, *Jefferson the Virginian* (Boston, Little, Brown and Co., 1948), 163, citing records on file in manuscript at the University of Virginia.

done and received the affection of his slaves in return.[3] Despite this, however, the Negroes at Shadwell and Monticello shared some of the less pleasant aspects of slavery in common with their fellows on other plantations. Though it is hard to imagine Jefferson employing the whip, Isaac tells us that the instrument was not unknown at Monticello:

Isaac knew of Colonel Cary mighty well. . . . He has given Isaac more whippings than he has fingers and toes. Mr. Jefferson used to set Isaac to open gates for Colonel Cary. . . . Whenever Isaac missed opening them gates in time, the Colonel soon as he get to the house, look about for him and whip him with his horsewhip.[4]

It appears that his slaves were not prone to attempts at escape. Yet, there is evidence that at least once Jefferson was forced to advertise in the Virginia *Gazette* offering a reward for a runaway.[5] Jefferson's Negroes obviously could expect good treatment in return for obedience and diligence, but even here, where their humanness was perhaps recognized more than on most plantations, they were primarily economic units, expected to add to the value of the land as did the crops and herds. One senses the position of the slave in a letter Jefferson wrote to John Taylor in which he discussed his plans to raise potatoes, clover and sheep. "The two former to feed every animal on the farm except my negroes, and the latter to feed them, diversified with rations of salted fish and molasses, both of them, wholesome, agreeable, and cheap articles of food." [6]

Jefferson was cognizant of the poor treatment afforded Negroes on other plantations, and when debts forced him to look toward his slaves as sources of cash, he was greatly disturbed. At one time he was compelled to lease his slaves for three years in order to hold his creditors at bay. He feared harsh treatment at the hands of temporary masters but reasoned that this short term expedient was better for his Negroes than putting them up for sale.[7] However, when economic necessity and the social amenities of Virginia plantation life required,

[3] Isaac, *Memoirs of a Monticello Slave* (Charlottesville, University of Virginia Press, 1951), 35-36, as dictated to Charles Campbell in the 1840's.
[4] *Ibid.*, 26.
[5] Julian P. Boyd (ed.), *The Papers of Thomas Jefferson* (Princeton, Princeton University Press, 1952), I, 33, citing Virginia *Gazette* (September 7, 1769).
[6] Albert Ellery Bergh (ed.), *The Writings of Thomas Jefferson* (Washington, D.C., The Thomas Jefferson Memorial Association, 1907), XVIII, 197 (December 29, 1794).
[7] Boyd, *The Papers of Jefferson*, XI, 640-41 and XIII, 343, To Nicholas Lewis (July 29, 1787 and June 11, 1788).

Jefferson took steps he obviously would have preferred to avoid. In 1793 he did sell some Negroes for the purpose of paying his creditors.[8] As befitted a man of his station Jefferson bequeathed "25 negroes little and big" to Thomas Mann Randolph as part of his daughter Martha's dowry.[9]

One gets the impression that Jefferson's contact with his slaves was indirect, depending upon managers like Nicholas Lewis and Francis Eppes, who familiarized themselves with the field hands. While at times in his letters Jefferson refers by name to Negroes, there is no evidence prior to his will of concern with the merits or vices of a particular slave.[10] Monticello appears to have been run like a modern business concern with a chain of command and even research facilities. Jefferson's directives regarding his slaves are similar to the memos from a chairman of the board to his personnel manager. There does not seem to have been the paternalistic approach and big family atmosphere that will be observed later when Andrew Jackson's Hermitage is examined.

Thomas Jefferson, the slave owner, was from his early manhood to the last year of his life an avowed foe of slavery. In his very first year in the House of Burgesses, 1769, Jefferson hurled two blows at the institution. The first, an attempt to convince the Burgesses to permit emancipation at the discretion of owners, failed; however, through his efforts, an anti-slave trade clause was included in the Virginia Non-importation Resolutions.[11] Similar clauses were inserted by Jefferson in the Virginia Non-importation Resolution of 1770, and in the Resolutions and Association of the Virginia Convention of 1774.[12]

There is some room to question whether Jefferson's activities in 1769 really indicate that he had at this point fully arrived at a strong anti-slavery position. Regarding his attempt to legislate manumission, Julian Boyd points out that, since the laws of George II prohibited such action, Jefferson's maneuver might have had as its purpose a

---

[8]   Paul Leicester Ford (ed.), *The Works of Thomas Jefferson* (New York and London, G. P. Putnam's Sons, 1892-1899), VI, 214, To James Lyle (April 15, 1793).

[9]   Boyd, *The Papers of Jefferson*, XVI, 154, To Thomas Mann Randolph (February 4, 1790).

[10]   Jefferson requested in his will that five slaves who had served him well be set free. Ford, *Works*, X, 395.

[11]   Jefferson's first effort is not recorded in the records of the Virginia legislature. He recalled the event in his autobiography, written in 1821; *ibid.*, I, 5.

[12]   Boyd, *Papers of Jefferson*, I, 44, 138.

protest against the King rather than a serious effort at emancipation.[13] Certainly the anti-slave trade clauses in the several non-importation resolutions were worded in a manner to suggest that their primary purpose was to damage Britain's trade and the monarch's status in the colonies. However, if one were to look for the source of Jefferson's views on slavery and indeed his faith in the Enlightenment, the logical beginning would be at Williamsburg during his student years. Of the three men, William Small, Francis Fauquier and George Wythe, who contributed so much in the shaping of the mind of young Jefferson, Fauquier and Wythe were particularly hostile toward slavery. It was in Wythe that Jefferson years later placed the hope for training future leaders hostile to black bondage.[14] A poem written into his copy of the *Virginia Almanack* for 1771 indicates that by this time Jefferson's sympathy for the Negro had been firmly established:

Inscription For an African Slave

Shores there are, bless'd shores for us remain,
And favor'd isles with golden fruitage crowns
Where tufted flow'rets paint the verdant plain,
Where ev'ry breeze shall med'cine every wound,
There the stern tyrant that embitters life,
Shall vainly suppliant spread his asking hand,
There shall we view the billow's raging strife,
And the kind breast, and waft his boat to land.[15]

The willingness of the Colonies to halt importation of slaves during the critical years prior to open warfare with the mother country very likely encouraged the optimism which Jefferson in 1774 expressed in his *A Summary View of the Rights of British America*. "The abolition of domestic slavery is the great object of desire in those colonies where it was unhappily introduced in their infant state." [16] That the statement caused no immediate furor in the Colonies was very likely due to Jefferson's comment that prior to such action it would first be "necessary to exclude all further importations from Africa".[17] Recognizing the propaganda value of the document and

---

[13] *Ibid.*, 30.
[14] *Ibid.*, VIII, 357, To Richard Price (August 7, 1785).
[15] Ford, *Works*, I, 391-92. Ford notes that a careful search had been made without finding the poem in print, and thus Jefferson has received credit as probable author. The handwriting on the almanack is Jefferson's.
[16] Boyd, *Papers of Jefferson*, I, 130.
[17] *Ibid.*

willing to go along in limiting the trade, those who had not the slightest desire to free their slaves obviously worried little about the young man's dream of the future.

The action of the Continental Congress in striking out the anti-slavery clause from the Declaration of Independence must have severely marred Jefferson's fond vision of the status of emancipation sentiment in the Colonies. Though this clause had blamed the King for introducing slavery, encouraging the slave trade and refusing to permit any limitation of that commerce, Jefferson's personal ire on July 2, 1776, was directed at the two states whose objections had caused the deletion, at Georgia and South Carolina "who had never attempted to restrain the importation of slaves, and who, on the contrary, still wished to continue it." Jefferson also placed part of the blame on northern "brethren" who saw their carrying trade threatened.[18]

The situation in Virginia was more promising. Jefferson had suc-ceeded in having a statement included in the Constitution adopted on June 29, 1776, condemning the King for his refusal to allow the exclusion of slavery.[19] On June 16, 1777, Jefferson won the greatest victory of his legislative war against the slave trade. His "Bill to Prevent the Importation of Slaves" could not be construed by anyone as merely another attack on the British throne. Its purposes were clearly stated: "To prevent more effectually the practise of holding persons in Slavery and importing them into this State. . . ." [20]

In addition to banning the external slave trade, the law permitted owners to manumit their slaves. An individual who desired to take such a step would not have freed himself entirely from responsibility for the actions of his former charges. The law provided that if any manumitted slave became a burden to society, the former owner or, in the case of his death, his executors or administrators would be compelled to reimburse to the parish the expenses of controlling the Negro.[21]

Though certainly not the primary purpose of this bill, the status and control of Negro freedmen was a major concern to Thomas Jefferson. He had indicate six months earlier that he did not equate

[18]   *Ibid.*, 314-15, citing Jefferson's *Notes of Proceedings of Continental Congress.*
[19]   *Ibid.*, 378.
[20]   *Ibid.*, II, 22. There is no conclusive evidence of Jefferson's authorship. He claimed authorship in his autobiography and most historians, including Boyd, accept it. As Boyd states, "Who else felt this way?"
[21]   *Ibid.*

legal equality with   reedom. His bill for establishing the
General Court stated,   r shall any Negro, Mulattoe, or Indian
be admitted to give e   but against or between Negroes, Mulattoes or Indians." [22] In   nary View and preamble to the Virginia
Constitution, Jefferson had expressed horror at the idea of the British
arming freed Negroes.[23] As governor he thought the law excluding
slaves from the militia very wise considering "the part of a Soldier's
Duty which consists of the Exercise of Arms".[24]

The most effective check placed on slavery in the United States
during the eigtheenth century was undoubtedly the anti-slavery
clause in the Northwest Ordinancer. Though Nathan Dane was the
author of the clause, Jefferson, in 1784, had made a major contribution which helped pave the way for such a step. As a member of the
committee appointed to prepare a plan for the temporary government of the Western Territory, he penned that body's recommendation that "after the year 1800 of the Christian era, there shall
be neither slavery nor involuntary servitude in any of the said
states . . .".[25]

As it turned out this was the last time Jefferson can be credited
with authorship of anti-slavery legislation. In 1776 he had successfully presented to the Virginia legislature his Bill for Revision of the
Laws. As chairman of the Committee of Revisions, which also included George Wythe, Edmund Pendleton, George Mason and
Thomas Lee, Jefferson was the primary spokesman for liberal reform
in Virginia between 1776 and 1786.[26] However, in the area of Negro
legislation the two bills drawn by Jefferson and presented to the
House of Delegates in 1785 could hardly be classified as humanitarian.
Their purposes were primarily to restrict contact between the races
and control the conduct of Negroes, particularly freed Negroes. The
first, Bill No. 51, "A Bill Concerning Slaves", was the more involved
and far-reaching of the two. It reiterated earlier limitations on the
importation of slaves, stating that any slave brought into the Com-

[22] Ibid., I, 633. Bill submitted on November 22, 1776, adopted on January 19,
1778.
[23] Ibid., 130 (Summary View, July, 1774), 378 (Constitution adopted on June
29, 1776).
[24] Ibid., V, 627, To the Speaker of the House of Delegates (May 10, 1781).
[25] Ibid., VI, 604-5. The report, submitted on March 1, 1784, was written
entirely in Jefferson's hand.
[26] Ibid., II, 313. Boyd cites Madison's acknowledgement of Jefferson's leadership in this work (Madison to S. H. Smith, November 4, 1826, D. L. C.,
Madison Papers).

monwealth would, after one year, be free. Negroes freed under this
provision were to leave the state within a year or be denied protection
of the law. Free Negroes entering the state of their own accord were
given twenty-four hours to leave or face the same consequences. Any
white woman bearing a Negro's child was also given a year's time
to leave the state with her baby. Whipping was designated as punishment for a slave travelling without a pass and for any Negro or
mulatto engaging in riots, unlawful assemblies, trespassing, or sedi-
tious speechmaking.[27] Commenting on this bill in his autobiography,
Jefferson recalled:

The bill on the subject of slaves was a mere digest of the existing laws
respecting them without any intimation of a plan for a future and general
emancipation. It was thought better that this should be kept back and
attempted only by way of amendement whenever the bill should be
brought on. The principles of the amendment, however, were agreed on,
that is to say the freedom of all born after a certain day, and deportation
at a proper age. But it was found that the public mind would not yet bear
the proposition. . . .[28]

This amendment was not presented to the legislature nor was Jefferson in the future to offer legislation leading to emancipation. Bill
No. 64, "A Bill for Proportioning Crimes and Punishments in Cases
Heretofore Capital", was also drawn by Jefferson. To the extent that
its provisions no longer demanded life or limb for certain crimes, the
bill certainly was humane. For the Negro slave, however, the bill
was discriminating and its punishments severe. For offenses punish-
able in the case of whites by hard labor, the slave was to be transported to the West Indies, South America or Africa, and be continued
in slavery. The bill was defeated by a single vote. However, the slave
provisions were not a factor in its failure.[29]

Within the content of the legislative proposals and comments made
by Jefferson in that decade, 1776-1786, there can be observed a
desire to halt the growth of slavery, particularly in Virginia, prevent
its expansion into new Territories, and inaugurate a plan for emancipation. Also observable is the belief that the most desirable place
for Negroes not under the firm control of white masters, freed

[27]   Ibid., 470-72. Jefferson's work on the Bill was completed in 1779, presented
to the legislature by Madison on October 31, 1785, and passed both houses on
December 9, 1785.
[28]   Ford, Works, I, 67-68.
[29]   Boyd, Papers of Jefferson, II, 504.

Negroes and criminals, was outside the nation. Equality under the law was to be denied Negroes in his "Bill for Establishing the General Court" and in Bill No. 51. In Bill no. 51 Jefferson indicated his disapproval of mixed issue, as he did when he affixed his signature to Bill No. 86 which prohibited marriage between freed men and slaves and whites and Negroes.[30]

Though these bills were not presented to the legislature until 1785, they had all been reported out of the Committee of Revisions by the end of 1779. In 1782 Jefferson completed his *Notes on the State of Virginia* in which the thought involved in his legislative proposals is clearly brought into focus. In this work Jefferson damned slavery as a blot on the nation, a political and moral evil. Emancipation was necessary in order to vindicate the liberty of human nature:

... can the liberties of a nation be thought secure when we have removed their only firm basis, a conviction in the minds of the people that these liberties are the gift of God? That they are not to be violated but with his wrath? Indeed I tremble for my country when I reflect that God is just: that his justice cannot sleep forever: that considering numbers, nature and natural means only, a revolution of the wheel of fortune, an exchange of situation, is among possible events: that it may become probable by supernatural interference![31]

Jefferson's approach seems primarily directed at engaging his reader's concern for national liberty and self-preservation, rather than an attempt to arouse a sense of pity or justice for the Negro. He warned the planters that slavery would destroy the morals and industry of their children.[32]

In the *Notes* Jefferson proposed an act be passed in the near future which would set free all slaves born after its passage. These children would remain with their parents until a "certain age" and then be trained by the state in agriculture, the arts, or sciences. At the age of eighteen for females and twenty-one for males, they were to be colonized. "It will probably be asked, Why not retain and incorporate the blacks into the state, and thus save the expense of supplying by importation of white settlers, the vacancies they will leave?" Jefferson answered

---

[30] *Ibid.*, 557. "A Bill Annulling Marriage Prohibited by the Levitical Law, and Appointing the Mode of Solemnizing Lawfull Marriage" was reported by the Committee of Revisions on June 18, 1779, presented by Madison on October 31, 1785, and died from inaction. Boyd attributes authorship to either Pendleton or Wythe.
[31] Ford, *Works*, III, 267.
[32] *Ibid.*, 266-67.

by pointing out the deep rooted prejudices entertained by the whites, the Negroes' memories of suffering, the possibilities of new provocations "and many other circumstances which will probably never end but in the extermination of one or the other race".[33]

These objections Jefferson termed political. To them he added others which he called physical and moral. Here Jefferson put aside the robes of a political thinker and employed his scientific mind to point out in great detail his reasons for believing that the Negro race was inferior to the white. He claimed the Negro to be inferior in terms of color. He wasn't quite sure where the blackness was located or whether it was caused by the color of the blood, the bile, or some other secretion. He was certain, however, that the difference was permanent and that it produced a color far less attractive than that of the Caucasians. He found distasteful "that immovable veil of black which covers all the emotions of the other race". To Jefferson, the flowing hair and "symmetry of form" of the whites were positive attractions missing in the Negro.[34]

It is amazing that a man of Jefferson's mental stature could not perceive that the Negro might have considered the color white equally unattractive. But it must be remembered that it was an eighteenth century Jefferson addressing an eighteenth century audience who wrote, "The circumstances of superior beauty is thought worth attention in the propagation of our horses, dogs, and others, why not in that of man?"[35]

In Jefferson's opinion another biological deficiency in the Negro was the "disagreeable odour" he produced. This, he explained, was caused by the fact that the Negro secretes less by the kidneys and more by the glands than does the white man. He also stated that the Negro required less sleep than the white, but did not use the time to any good purpose. Jefferson recognized certain praiseworthy characteristics and abilities which he credited as peculiar to the Negro race, but in general, he left the impression that they lacked the higher mental attributes necessary to advance their race to a level equal to the whites:

They are at least as brave, and more adventuresome. But this may perhaps proceed from a want of forethought, which prevents their seeing a danger till it be present. When present they do not go through with it with more

33 *Ibid.*, 243-44.
34 *Ibid.*, 244.
35 *Ibid.*

coolness or steadiness than the whites. They are more ardent after their female, but love seems with them to be more an eager desire than a tender delicate mixture of sentiment and sensation.[36]

He stated that the Negro appeared to "participate more in sensation than reflection". Thus, though they are equal to the white in memory, "they are inferior in reason, and dull, tasteless, anomalous" in imagination.[37]

Jefferson acknowledged that the Negro was generally more gifted than the white in music, but as yet not having proved his ability in the more complicated forms of composition and melody.[38] Obviously, he was again setting the Negro's accomplishments in this art against the standards of white Western Civilization, failing to recognize the possibilty of new, different and creditable African forms.

In the field of literature, also, he pictured the accomplishments of Negroes as far inferior to those of white authors. He called Phyllis Wheatley's works "below the dignity of criticism". Ignatio Sancho was placed by Jefferson on the top of the list of Negro writers, but in a class far below even the mediocre authors of the white race:

... his letters do more honour to the heart than the head. They breathe the purest effusions of friendship and general philanthropy and show how great a degree of the latter may be compounded with strong religious zeal. He is often happy in the turn of his compliments, affects a Shandean fabrication of words. But his imagination is wild and extravagant, escapes incessantly from every restraint of reason and taste.[39]

It is interesting to note that Phyllis Wheatley in 1773 and Ignatio Sancho in 1782 had their complete works published in London, a feat rare even among whites in the New World at this time.[40] However, as a child of the Enlightenment, Jefferson's dislike for romantic fancy is understandable.

Jefferson displayed a degree of compassion toward the Negro in stating that, if the race lacked endowments of the head, it was rich in those of the heart. He attributed a disposition to theft to the fact that "a man in whose favour no laws of property exist, probably feels himself less bound to respect those made in favour of others." But,

[36] *Ibid.*, 245.
[37] *Ibid.*
[38] *Ibid.*, 246.
[39] *Ibid.*
[40] *Ibid.*, ed. no. pp. 246-47.

alas, the scientist could not let this stand unqualified, for he then proceeded to mention the numerous instances of integrity among Roman and Grecian slaves. "But the slaves of which Homer speaks were white." [41] It appears that Jefferson suffered under the misconception that Roman and Grecian slaves were exclusively white. He also failed to take into consideration the fact that the slaves to whom Homer referred often came from civilizations on a level with the Greek and that the slaves of Rome, particularly those from the areas of Hellenic culture, in many cases surpassed their masters in learning. Thus he reasoned that, because Roman slaves were white, emancipation was a rather simple matter, lacking the complications that would arise in America. "The slave, when made free, might mix with, without staining, the blood of his master. But with us a second is necessary, unknown to history. When freed, he is to be removed beyond the reach of mixture." [42]

Jefferson made it clear to his readers that much research had yet to be undertaken before definite conclusions could be reached concerning the status of the Negro race. He advanced it, therefore, "as a suspicion only, that the blacks, whether originally a distinct race, or made distinct by time and circumstances are inferior to the whites in the endowments of body and mind." [43] The discussion of the Negro and slavery was closed on a rather optimistic note:

I think a change is already perceptible, since the origin of the present revolution. The spirit of the master is abating, that of the slave rising from the dust, his condition mollifying, the way I hope preparing, under the auspices of heaven for a total emancipation. . . . [44]

This combination of a fervent desire to see the slaves freed along with the belief that the Negro was a member of an inferior race remained the basis of Jefferson's life-long pronouncements advocating emancipation followed by expatriation.

The year 1785 marked the culmination of Jefferson's efforts as chairman of the Committee of Revisors. It saw the first printing of his *Notes on the State of Virginia.* However, the year was also significant in a less positive respect. Though Jefferson continued to advocate emancipation, he no longer offered public advice or strong private support for its accomplishment. Furthermore, Jefferson's

[41] *Ibid.,* 249.
[42] *Ibid.*
[43] *Ibid.,* 250.
[44] *Ibid.,* 267-68.

thoughts about slavery and emancipation appear to have been more and more conditioned by factors other than his belief in the natural right of freedom and concern over the immorality of the institution. For one thing, he seems to have become aware of the fact that anti-slavery feeling was not making the strides which he earlier had envisioned. In this year, 1785, we have his first reference to the rising generation, rather than his own, as offering the best hope for anti-slavery action. He felt that the "sacred side" was "gaining daily recruits from the influx into office of young men grown and growing up". He also expected much from the students of George Wythe, whose sentiments on the subject of slavery he termed "unequivocal".[45]

The realization that his views on slavery might turn a large segment of mature public opinion against him caused Jefferson to take great pains to insure that the printed copies of his *Notes* got into the hands of only those who would appreciate and sympathize with them. In June of 1785, from Paris, he wrote letters in which his fears were expressed. To Chastellux he confided, "I have printed and reserved just enough copies to be able to give one to every young man at the college. It is to them I look, to the rising generation, and not to the one now in power for these great reformations." [46]

Jefferson had asked Madison to sound out public opinion in order to determine what kind of reception the *Notes* would be given in Virginia. Madison's reply indicated the strong personal support he gave to Jefferson's plans for emancipation, but also made it quite clear that, by 1785, anyone who valued public support for future political endeavors had better be extremely cautious about making statements attacking slavery. This is made strikingly evident by the fact that portions of the letter in italics below were originally written in code. In referring to the *Notes*, Madison wrote:

I have looked them over carefully myself and consulted several judicious friends in confidence. We are all sensible that the *freedom* of your stricture on some *particular measures* and *opinions* will displeasure *their* respective abettors. But we equally concur in thinking that this consideration ought not to be weighed against the *utility of your plan*. We think both the facts and remarks which you have assembled too valuable not to be made known, at least to those for whom *you destined them*, and speak of them

[45] Boyd, *Papers of Jefferson*, VIII, 357, To Richard Price (August 7, 1785). Price had sent Jefferson a number of anti-slavery tracts he had written.
[46] *Ibid.*, 184, To Chastellux (June 7, 1785). He also told Monroe (*Ibid.*, 229, June 17, 1785) and Charles Thompson (*Ibid.*, 245, June 21, 1785) of his fears of publishing.

to one another in terms which I must not repeat to you. Mr. Wythe suggested that it might be better to put the number you may allot to the University in the library, rather than to distribute them among the Students. In the latter case the Stock will be immediately exhausted. In the former, the discretion of the professor will make it serve the Students as they successively come in. Perhaps too, an *indiscriminate gift* might offend *some narrow minded parents.*[47]

Jefferson's reply indicates clearly that, in addition to being a humanitarian and scientist, he was an astute politician, not prone to throwing caution to the wind. He thanked Madison for his information and assured his friend that his advice would be followed. Jefferson's uneasiness about the matter, which he referred to as "this trifle", is evident. He told Madison that he had distributed a few copies to confidants in Paris, "writing in every copy a restraint against its publication". It seems one of these people had since died and Jefferson wrote, "I immediately took every precaution I could to recover this copy." [48]

In the years following the publication of his *Notes*, Jefferson's published papers record the receipt of only two letters in which his views on the Negro, as expressed in the work, were discussed. Neither would tend to encourage anything but caution. From New York, David Ramsey wrote of his admiration for Jefferson's opposition to slavery but took issue with his racial theories.[49] In 1789, Francis Kinlock of South Carolina told Jefferson of the "general alarm" occasioned by his views. "It is not easy to get rid of old prejudices, and the word 'emancipation' operates like an apparition upon a South Carolina planter." [50]

During the years 1786 through 1790, Jefferson evidently put aside his elaborate emancipation schemes and was satisfied with making infrequent and vague attacks upon slavery and seemingly half-hearted suggestions for its melioration and elimination. He continued to be cautious about the dissemination of his anti-slavery views, refusing membership in a French abolition society on the grounds that since

[47] *Ibid.*, IX, 38 (November 15, 1785). Reference to Jefferson's inquiry is found in his letter to James Monroe dated June 17, 1785; *ibid.*, VIII, 229.
[48] *Ibid.*, IX, 264-65 (February 8, 1786).
[49] *Ibid.*, 441 (May 3, 1786). Ramsey wrote, "I believe all mankind to be originally the same and only diversified by accidental circumstances. I flatter myself that in a few centuries the negro will lose their [sic] black color. I think now they are less black in Jersey than Carolina, their lips less thick, their noses less flat."
[50] *Ibid.*, XV, 72 (April 26, 1789).

"those whom I serve having never yet been able to give their voice against this practise, it is decent for me to avoid too public a demonstration of my wishes to see it abolished." He stated that membership in such a society in France might impair his work toward the goal at home.[51]

In three letters during this period, Jefferson expressed an interest in economic approaches to the slavery problem. To John Rutledge, Jr., he offered the observation that the olives he had seen in France and Italy would be ideal crops for South Carolina, providing a practical means of "bettering the condition" of the slaves.[52] To Benjamin Vaughn he urged the substitution of maple sugar for cane sugar. "What a blessing to substitute a sugar which requires only the labor of children for that which it is said renders the slavery of the blacks necessary."[53] Writing from Paris, he told Edward Bancroft of an experiment he contemplated for Monticello:

I shall endeavor to import as many Germans as I have grown slaves. I will settle them and my slaves on farms of 50 acres each, intermingled, and place all on the footing of the metayers mediantani of Europe. Their children shall be brought up as others are in habits of property and foresight, and I have no doubts they will need government; with these all that can be done is to oblige them to labor as the laboring poor of Europe do, and to apply to their comfortable subsistence the produce of their labor, retaining such a moderate portion of it as may be a just equivalent for the use of the lands they labor and the stock and other necessary advances.[54]

Three plans worthy of consideration, but maple sugar did not replace cane sugar; olives did not become part of the slaves' diet in South Carolina, and Jefferson did not import his Germans. Strong public declarations against slavery had given way in time to plans for emancipation intended for the eyes of a chosen few, and the latter had given way to these seemingly off-the-cuff flights of fancy expressed in three private communications. The flames of Jefferson's antislavery passion appear to have diminished to a glowing ember by the end of 1790.

In 1791 the beginning of a revived interest in slavery is apparent in Secretary of State Jefferson's letters. It was an interest motivated in large part by fear; fear of Florida as a haven for runaway slaves,

[51] Ibid., XII, 577, To Brissot de Warville (February 11, 1788).
[52] Ibid., XIII, 263 (June 19, 1788).
[53] Ibid., XVI, 579 (June 27, 1790).
[54] Ibid., XIV, 492 (January 26, 1789).

fear of the impact of the slave revolts in Santo Domingo and elsewhere on the slaves of his own land. He wrote to the governor of
Florida, reminding him of the Spanish sovereign's order closing the
Florida border to runaway slaves from America and added, "... we
trust that your Excellency will permit, and aid the recovery of persons of the same description who have heretofore taken refuge within
your government." [55] The same year Jefferson urged the President
to ignore the petitions for entry from a group of free people of color
from Grenada on the grounds that they were parties to a domestic
quarrel in which the United States could not justifiably involve itself.
To this legal position Jefferson added his personal opinion that it
would not be desirable "to draw a body of sixty thousand free blacks
and mulattoes into our country".[56]

In 1793 the situation in Santo Domingo caused Jefferson to display
real concern. The fear of slave revolt in America was added to, and
surpassed in intensity, his other arguments for emancipation and
expatriation. To Monroe he wrote regarding this subject, "It is high
time we should forsee the bloody scenes which our children certainly,
and possibly ourselves (south of the Potomac) will have to wade
through, and try to avert them." [57] Jefferson sent a note warning the
Governor of South Carolina of the possibility of a slave insurrection
excited by refugees from Santo Domingo.[58] It is interesting to note
that in the same year Jefferson, who had earlier been repelled by
the idea, sold some Negroes to pay his debts.[59]

The slavery problem appears to have gradually receded to a status
in Jefferson's mind not greatly different from Adams' view of the
Indian problem. With the threat of Santo Domingo no longer immediately present, the issue of slavery disappeared from Jefferson's
writings. There is only one reference to it among the published
works of Jefferson for the years 1794 to 1800. In 1797 he told St. George
Tucker that Santo Domingo could be a prelude of what might happen
in the United States if a plan was not devised and put into action of
freeing and getting rid of the Negroes.[60]

In 1800 Jefferson wrote a letter to Governor James Monroe in
which he pondered over the question of what should be done to

[55] Ford, *Works*, V, 296 (January 26, 1791).
[56] *Ibid.*, 342 (June 20, 1791).
[57] *Ibid.*, VI, 349 (July 14, 1793).
[58] Bergh, *Writings of Jefferson*, IX, 275-76 (December 23, 1793).
[59] Ford, *Works*, VI, 214, To James Lyle (April 15, 1793).
[60] *Ibid.*, VII, 168 (August 28, 1797).

punish those who might take part in a slave insurrection like that of
Santo Domingo. He stood opposed to hanging or any punishment in-
flicted in a mood of revenge which went "one step beyond necessity".
The rationale Jefferson offered for this position was not founded on
the rights of humanity or the morals of Virginia's children but on the
fear that unduly harsh punishment would cause "the other states and
the world at large" to "forever condemn" Virgina. He offered the
idea of immediate exportation, suggesting that Monroe encourage
the legislature to pass a law requiring such action in the event of a
slave revolt in the State. "Our situation is indeed a difficult one:
for I doubt whether these people can ever be permitted to go at
large among us in safety. To reprieve them and keep them in prison
till the meeting of the legislature would encourage efforts for their
release." Jefferson urged Monroe to keep the contents of the letter
a secret.[61]

The abortive Gabriel Prosser insurrection, which Jefferson referred
to as "the tragedy of 1800", had greatly disturbed Governor Monroe
and the Virginia legislature.[62] Jefferson's advice evidently was influential in Monroe's suggesting to the legislature the idea of a plan
for the resettlement of criminal Negroes.[63] President Jefferson kept
close tabs on the plan's progress in Virginia and, during the years
of his first term, quietly used his executive influence to investigate
various possible locations for resettlement. On November 24, 1801,
Jefferson informed Monroe of what he considered to be the proper
scope of the resettlement bill. "This should be for special crimes,
conspiracy, insurgency, treason, rebellion." He declared himself
strongly opposed to colonization in western territory, even on land
owned by Britain and Spain:

However our present interest may restrain us within our own limits. It is
impossible not to look forward to distant times, when our rapid multiplica-
tion will expand itself beyond those limits and cover the whole northern
if not the southern continent, with a people speaking the same language,
governed in similar forms, and by similar laws; nor can we contemplate
with satisfaction either blot or mixture on that surface.[64]

Having added the cause of nationalism to the necessities of science
and humanitarianism to support his position on expatriation, Jeffer-

[61] *Ibid.*, 457-58 (September 20, 1800).
[62] Jefferson referred to the revolt in these terms in a letter to Monroe; *ibid.*,
VIII, 104 (November 24, 1801).
[63] *Ibid.*, 103. From James Monroe (November 17, 1801).
[64] *Ibid.*, 104-5.

son suggested looking into South America and the West Indies. Santo Domingo appeared particularly attractive:

... the blacks are established into a sovereignty de facto, and have organized themselves under regular law and government. I should conjecture that their present ruler might be willing, on many considerations, to receive even that description which would be exiled for acts deemed criminal by us, but meritorious, perhaps, by him.[65]

It appears that the man who provided the great words of 1776 to justify revolution in the name of freedom was now ready to admit the existence of varying interpretation of that right. Unlike the ruler of Santo Domingo, Jefferson considered that attempts by the Negroes to gain freedom through revolt were criminal acts. Jefferson's expressed interest in this project was not motivated by a desire to emancipate the slaves, but rather to rid the nation of those slaves who had attempted, or in the future might attempt, to free themselves. Fear for the safety of his white neighbors and dreams of future national glory appear to have worked the greatest influence on Jefferson's thinking at this time.

Jefferson promised Monroe that he would sound out the government of any territory in which Virginia was interested for such a project. Still extremely cautious about having his feelings on even this aspect of the slavery problem made public, he urged Monroe to limit discussion of his views to members of the legislature. "Their publication might have an ill effect in more than one quarter. In confidence of attention to this I shall indulge in greater freedom in writing." [66]

The Virginia legislature resolved, on January 23, 1802, to ask the President to look into areas in Africa or South America as possible resettlement areas for insurgent Negroes.[67] Jefferson concurred with the recommendation and mentioned particular interest in Britain's colony of Sierra Leone. He told Monroe that if profitable commercial arrangements could be worked out with that territory, it might provide an economically feasible method of resettling free as well as criminal Negroes. However, he urged Monroe not to ignore the West Indies and South America "so as to have some other resource provided if the one most desirable should be unattainable." [68]

[65]   *Ibid.,* 105.
[66]   *Ibid.,* 103.
[67]   Jefferson referred to this act in a letter to Monroe; *ibid.,* 152 (June 2, 1802).
[68]   *Ibid.,* 152-54 (June 2, 1802).

Jefferson instructed his minister to Great Britain, Rufus King, to discover the British reaction to the Sierra Leone scheme, making it explicit that this was an official request from the legislature of Virginia via its governor, James Monroe.[69] The Portuguese government was also approached on the possibility of obtaining territory in Brazil for the project. The inquiries came to naught. Both governments considered the Negroes in their territories enough to handle without inviting insurgent blacks from the United States.[70] There is no evidence of the rulers of Santo Domingo being approached on the question.

Recognizing regulation of the slave trade to be within his jurisdictional power as President, and very likely also recognizing that public opinion supported his views on the traffic, Jefferson did not hesitate to use the influence of his office to destroy that form of commerce. In cases brought to his attention involving infractions of the existing laws, he demanded punishment. To Gallatin he stated, "The traffic ... is so odious that no indulgence can be claimed." [71] Regarding a slaver named Captain Ingerham, Jefferson wrote:

He petitions for a pardon, as does his wife on behalf of herself, her children, and his mother. His situation as far as respects himself, merits no commiseration; that of his wife, children, and mother, suffering from want of his aid does: so also does the condition of the unhappy human beings who he forcibly brought away from their native country, and whose wives, children, and parents are now suffering from want of their aid and comfort.[72]

Jefferson refused the pardon. However, for the sake or Ingerham's family, he ordered him kept under a law which would confine him for two years, rather than one which demanded life imprisonment.[73]

In his Sixth Annual Message on December 2, 1806, Jefferson reminded Congress of the approach of the year in which the slave trade could be constitutionally excluded from the country. Referring to the trade as "those violations of human rights which have been so long continued on the unoffending inhabitants of Africa, and

---

[69] *Ibid.*, 161-63 (July 13, 1802).
[70] Jefferson recalled his attempts in a letter to John Lynch on January 21, 1811; *ibid.*, IX, 303-4.
[71] *Ibid.*, VIII, 106 (November 28, 1801).
[72] *Ibid.*, 231, To Christopher Ellery (May 19, 1803).
[73] *Ibid.*, 232.

which the morality, the reputation, the best interests of our country have been eager to proscribe", Jefferson told the legislators that it was not too early to impede the traffic by warning planners of long expeditions that they might very well run afoul of the law if their voyages were not completed before 1808.[74]

The tone of Jefferson's speech was almost exuberant. He no doubt was certain that the year 1808 would see the end of legal sanction of the slave trade. However, at the same time, concerning the possibility of the emancipation of the slaves in the near future, he was quite pessimistic. In 1805 he told William A. Burwell that he had given up the idea of any early provisions for the extinguishment of slavery. Morality had proven an ineffective argument. He placed his hopes on economic interests. The lowering value of slaves might some day unwittingly serve humanity's cause. The man who so feared the consequences of slave revolts was fully cognizant of the possibility that such upheavals could also hasten the day of Negro freedom:

Interest is therefore preparing the disposition to be just; and this will be goaded from time to time by the insurrectionary spirits of the slaves. This is easily quelled in its first efforts; but from being local it will become general, and whenever it does it will rise more formidable after every defeat, until we shall be forced, after dreadful scenes and sufferings, to release them in their own way, which without sufferings we might now model after our own convenience.[75]

In another letter the same year President Jefferson told his correspondent that the question of procuring German emigrants to replace Negro slaves was purely a matter for the legislature of the states, the federal government "possessing no powers but those enumerated in the constitution". Jefferson admitted having "often thought on the subject you propose", but he offered little hope for the possibility of its implementation. "I not only doubt, but despair of their [state legislature] taking up this operation, till some strong pressure of circumstances shall force it on them."[76]

Thus Jefferson, who once considered a scheme for importing Germans for Monticello, now laid the responsibility for such action in the hands of the state legislators. One cannot take issue with his denial of federal authority in this area; however, the failure of Jeffer-

[74]   Ibid., 492-93.
[75]   Ibid., 340-41 (January 28, 1805).
[76]   Ibid., 402-3, To J. P. Reibelt (December 21, 1805).

son to mention the details of his earlier plan and the absence of any suggestion of personal involvement adds to the impression that he was no longer offering leadership on the issue.

Jefferson had earlier backed away from an active association with avowed abolitionists. In rejecting membership in a French society in 1788, he had claimed that participation endangered the cause of emancipation at home. In 1805 Jefferson received a letter from Thomas Brannagan, author of an anti-slavery work published in Philadelphia that year. Brannagan requested that Jefferson add his name to the list of subscribers. The President could neither bring himself to accept Brannagan's request nor see his way clear to answer his letter. He asked Dr. George Logan to explain to Brannagan that he felt such a small step could accomplish little and would irritate many whose support he sought for other measures. He told Logan, "Should an occasion ever occur in which I can interpose with decisive effects, I shall certainly know and do my duty with promptitude and zeal." [77]

Probably Jefferson would have done just that. He had set forth his stand on slavery time and again — emancipation with expatriation. There is no evidence that he seriously considered the possibility of the first step unless accompanied by the second. Therefore Jefferson can never be considered to have been an abolitionist in the terms usually associated with that movement. His plan, with its elaborate scheme for freeing and training the potential expatriate, could not have been achieved without a great measure of Southern initiative and support. It was, therefore, to the South that he looked first with hope and later with growing despair. In his earlier years he had indicated a willingness to help lead a Southern emancipation movement. This not only became a man of the Enlightenment, but it appeared to Jefferson at the time to be a cause in which a Virginia politician might engage with hopes for a large measure of public support.

Jefferson the President does not appear to have been vastly different from the author of the Declaration of Independence. He was still the humanitarian of old. Politics, however, had changed. The cotton gin and, to some extent, the threat of slave revolts had worked enduring effects on the Southern view of slavery. Jefferson recognized this. He was still the politician of old. As a man who hoped to attain many ends by political means, he obviously was not willing to

[77] *Ibid.*, 351-52 (May 11, 1805).

sacrifice all for the dubious possibility of the achievement of one. He was not willing to lead an anti-slavery crusade against the section from which he had drawn his greatest political support. Nor, evidently, was he willing to risk economic ruin to the South as the cost of emancipation. Thus, the same Jefferson who awaited with eager anticipation the year 1808 and with it the end of the slave trade, suggested in 1807, in answer to pleas of residents, that Louisiana, which had been prohibited from importing slaves from any source, be allowed by action of Congress to obtain slaves from other states.[78]

During the ten years between James Madison's entry into the White House and the Missouri statehood question which terminated "The Era of Good Feelings", Thomas Jefferson wrote a number of letters in which the problems of slavery were discussed. In them Jefferson repeated his conviction that the slaves would eventually be freed either by the generosity of the master or "by the bloody process of St. Domingo".[79] The best hope, he continued to believe, was voluntary emancipation, followed by training and colonization. He looked with favor on attempts to have Congress purchase land on the coast of Africa for the voluntary emigration of Negroes, stating that Federal action "may be the cornerstone of this future edifice".[80]

The hope which Jefferson expressed in these letters was tempered by a large measure of disappointment. To Edward Coles' plea that he assume leadership in the emancipation struggle Jefferson replied, "This, my dear sir, is like bidding old Priam to buckle the armor of Hector.... No, I have overlived the generation with which mutual labors and perils begat mutual confidence and influence. This enterprise is for the young: for those who can follow it up, and bear it through to its consummation." [81] Though placing the responsibility on the shoulders of the young, Jefferson was far from optimistic about their willingness to assume the burden. "I have not perceived the growth of this disposition in the rising generation, of which I once had sanguine hopes. I leave it, therefore, to time...." [82]

That Jefferson felt slavery would not in the near future leave the Southern scene is indicated in a letter which he wrote to Dr. Thomas Cooper in 1814. He informed his English correspondent that the condition of the slave in America was not much worse than that of

---

[78] Bergh, *Writings of Jefferson*, XI, 135, To John Dickinson (January 13, 1807).
[79] Ford, *Works*, IX, 478, To Edward Coles (August 25, 1814).
[80] *Ibid.*, X, 77, To Dr. Thomas Humphreys (February 8, 1817).
[81] *Ibid.*, IX, 479 (August 24, 1814).
[82] *Ibid.*, X, 77, To Dr. Thomas Humphreys (August 7, 1825).

the English laborer or seaman. In his closing paragraph Jefferson emphasized that he was by no means justifying slavery, but merely engaging in a comparison.[83] The letter could not have led Dr. Cooper to feel that Jefferson was "going soft" on slavery, and there is nothing to lead today's reader to such a conclusion. However, what is significant to one who has examined the various letters Jefferson wrote to foreigners is the contrast in tone between this letter and his earlier statements to men like Chastellux. Gone are the declarations of faith in a younger generation raised on the milk of humanitarian enlightenment.

The Jefferson of these years was a man in retirement. His letters, for the most part, reflect a mind involved in reflection and contemplation. The Missouri crisis quickly altered this situation. As Jefferson stated in his famous letter to John Holmes:

I had for a long time ceased to read newspapers, or pay any attention to public affairs, confident they were in good hands, and content to be a passenger in our bark to the shore from which I am not distant. But this momentous question, like a fire bell in the night, awakened and filled me with terror.[84]

The terror he expressed was caused by the fear that the Union's very survival was in danger. As he told John Adams, "From the battle of Bunker's Hill to the treaty of Paris we never had so ominous a question."[85] The terror, which was a mark of his nationalism, was accompanied by the anger of a politician and the hope of an opponent of slavery. Jefferson labeled the Missouri crisis as a "mere party trick". The Federalists, he claimed, were "taking advantage of the virtuous feelings of the people to effect a division of parties by a geographical line . . .".[86] Jefferson left no doubt as to where he stood. If the Union was to fall over the issue, it was because the position taken in the North was unconstitutional. He stated that the power "to regulate the condition of the different description of men composing a State . . . is the exclusive right of every State, which nothing in the Constitution has taken from them and given to the General Government."[87]

[83] Bergh, *Writings of Jefferson,* XIV, 183-84 (September 10, 1814).
[84] Ford, *Works,* X, 157 (April 22, 1820).
[85] *Ibid.,* 152 (December 10, 1819).
[86] Bergh, *Writings of Jefferson,* XV, 280, To Charles Pinckney (September 30, 1820).
[87] Ford, *Works,* X, 158, To John Holmes (April 22, 1820).

Jefferson expressed to Albert Gallatin the belief that the evils of the crisis were accompanied by "one good effect". He believed that some plan of general emancipation and deportation would be recognized as a necessity and again mentioned the plan first suggested in his *Notes*, specifying Santo Domingo as the most likely spot for colonization.[88] Earlier in the year Jefferson had declared that the expansion of slavery into new territories or states was in itself not an evil, but rather a potential good:

Of one thing I am certain, that as the passage of slaves from one State to another would not make a slave of a single human being who would not be so without it, so their diffusion over a greater surface would make them individually happier and proportionally facilitate the accomplishment of their emancipation, by dividing the burthen on a greater number of coadjutors.[89]

Though Jefferson referred to the benefits of diffusion at least once again in 1823, it is interesting to note that he did not mention it in his letter to Gallatin.[90] Perhaps he realized that Gallatin might have been rather surprised that the man who had been so determined to block slavery's expansion into the Northwest Territory in 1784 could now envision diffusion as hastening the day of emancipation. If James Monroe heard these views of Jefferson, he too might have been bewildered. Had not Jefferson in 1802 urged him to put aside the possibility of resetting criminal Negroes in the western lands on the grounds that our general population would some day expand into that territory upon whose surface could not be contemplated "with satisfaction, either blot or mixture"?[91]

It appears that in introducing the diffusion concept into his views on emancipation, Jefferson was primarily concerned with providing a humanitarian argument to support a politically expedient position. His enthusiasm for the idea, it seems, was limited in time to the period of the Missouri conflict and in scope to only two letters. He had not referred to it before and was not to mention it again after 1823.

The fact that Jefferson would take such a position does not really diminish his stature as a champion of emancipation. It does, however,

[88]   *Ibid.*, 178 (December 26, 1820).
[89]   *Ibid.*, 158, To John Holmes (April 22, 1820).
[90]   Jefferson spoke of diffusion and Santo Domingo in a letter to William Short; Bergh, *Writings of Jefferson*, XV, 469-70 (September 8, 1823).
[91]   Ford, *Works*, VIII, 105 (November 24, 1801).

help to place the anti-slavery cause in its proper relative position among Jefferson's concerns. Concern for the moral, political, and economic welfare of his state, section, and nation, and concern for the purity of his race undoubtedly affected and took precedence over his desire to see the Negroes freed. These concerns are evident in his plan for emancipation and they were implicit in his refusal to allow his position as an advocate of emancipation to endanger his political career.

Among the published writings of Jefferson there is a letter regarding slavery for each of the three years preceding his death on July 4, 1826. In all of them he reaffirmed his conviction that slavery must and would some day be eliminated. He told Jared Sparks in 1824 that a colonization plan in Africa was a fine experiment to prove the Negroes capable of being self-sufficient.[92] He encouraged Fanny Wright in 1825 to attempt to prove the same thing in her proposed Negro communal settlement.[93] He agreed with William Short in 1826 that placing the Negroes in a condition of serfdom was better than continuing to hold them as slaves.[94] However, he made it clear in each case that these plans were suitable as experiments only. In his letter to Jared Sparks he restated his conviction that the plan set forth in his *Notes* was the best hope for a final solution and added that Santo Domingo was undoubtedly the ideal location for resettlement.[95] In each of these last three lettters Jefferson was replying to queries and suggestions directed to him. He himself had long given up the initiative. As he told Short, "On the subject of emancipation I have ceased to think because it is not to be a work of my day ... I repeat my abandonment of the subject." [96]

Jefferson's biographers have not failed to note his expressions of hostility toward slavery. They have enumerated the various efforts he made during the Revolutionary War era to deal the institution devastating blows. However, in addition to a failure of the authors to follow Jefferson's thought and deeds regarding slavery into his later years, many have neglected to describe Jefferson's plans for expatriation and have either failed to mention or have given a rather softened view of his strong suspicion that the Negro race was mentally and physically inferior to the white. Bernard Mayo, for example,

92   *Ibid.,* X, 290 (February 4, 1824).
93   *Ibid.,* 344 (August 7, 1825).
94   *Ibid.,* 362 (January 18, 1826).
95   *Ibid.,* 290-92 (February 4, 1824).
96   *Ibid.,* 362 (January 18, 1826).

offers a section of Jefferson's letter to Edward Coles in 1814, in which Jefferson assured his reader that emancipation must come.[97] The author failed to note in any way the remainder of the letter in which Jefferson expressed the necessity for expatriation since "amalgamation produces degradation".[98]

Saul Padover referred to Jefferson's racial views in a rather round-about fashion, stating, "Many, possibly most, white people insisted that Negroes were inferior being in every way, and hence it was 'natural' that they be enslaved. Jefferson had strong doubts about the 'natural' inferiority of Negroes." He went on to state that Jefferson told the Negro mathematician Benjamin Banneker that he realized that the so-called inferiority of colored people was due to their environment, that they had not been given a chance to raise themselves above their degraded status.[99] What Jefferson actually wrote in 1791 was:

Nobody wishes more than I do to see such proofs as you exhibit that nature has given to our black brethren talents equal to those of the other colors of men and that the appearance of a want of them is owing merely to a degraded condition of their existence both in Africa and America.[100]

Other authors have also employed Jefferson's enthusiasm for Banneker's achievements as expressed in his letters to the Negro and to the Marquis De Condorcet to provide an example of his open mind on the question of race.[101] However, these were not very good choices. Jefferson appears to have been either a bit insincere in his flattery or to have had second thoughts on the matter as the years passed. In 1809 Jefferson told Joel Barlow about a letter he had received from Bishop Gregoire. Jefferson accused Gregoire of being overly credulous regarding stories of Negro equality, of gathering up "every story he could find of men of color (without distinguishing whether black or of what degree of mixture) however slight the mention or light the authority on which they are quoted." [102] He then referred to Banneker, whose accomplishments he had earlier praised as ex-

[97] Bernard Mayo, *Jefferson Himself* (Boston, Houghton Mifflin Co., 1942), 293.
[98] Ford, *Works*, IX, 478 (August 25, 1814).
[99] Saul K. Padover, *Jefferson* (New York, Harcourt Brace and Co., 1942), 233-34.
[100] Ford, *Works*, V, 377-78 (August 30, 1791).
[101] See Malone, *Jefferson the Virginian*, 268; John Dos Passos, *The Head and Heart of Thomas Jefferson* (Garden City, New York, Doubleday and Company, 1954), 387-88.
[102] Ford, *Works*, X, 261 (October 8, 1809).

amples which might eventually help prove theories of Negro inferiority to be unjustified:

The whole do not amount, in point of evidence, to what we know ourselves of Banneker. We know he had spherical trigonometry enough to make almanacs, but not without the suspicion of aid from Ellicot, who was his neighbor and friend, and never missed an opportunity of puffing him. I have a long letter from Banneker, which shows him to have had a mind of very common stature indeed.[103]

On the question of the position of the Negro as a race Jefferson maintained throughout his life the views expressed in the *Notes on the State of Virginia*. Though denying infallibility and proclaiming that he was ready and eager to be shown otherwise, he nonetheless did not desert his opinion that the Negro was inferior. Even in letters to abolitionists, while encouraging and supporting their endeavors, he gave no impression that his earlier attitude had been altered. In his oft-quoted letter to Henri Gregoire, he tried to impress upon the Bishop the fact that the views in his *Notes* were far from fixed. However, nowhere in this, what Jefferson termed, "very soft answer", was there evidence of a changed position on the Negro, only strong reassurances that he was quite prepared to be convinced otherwise.[104] A letter to Fanny Wright in 1825 had a similar tone. "We are not sufficiently acquainted with all the nations of Africa to say that there may not be some in which habits of industry are established, and the arts practiced which are necessary to render life comfortable." [105] It is interesting to note that, in the letters to Gregoire and Wright, Jefferson alluded to a rather obvious shortcoming in his original observations of the Negro, that they were made "in the limited sphere of" his "own state, where the opportunities for the development of their genius were not favorable and those of exercising it still less so".[106]

Whether these statements indicate a growing self-criticism of his earlier statements regarding the Negro's mental and physical capacities, it is difficult to say. It must be remembered to whom these letters were addressed. What remains a fact is that Jefferson never

[103] *Ibid.*
[104] *Ibid.*, IX, 246 (February 25, 1809). In his letter to Joel Barlow (October 8, 1809), Jefferson referred to his "very soft answer" to Gregoire; *ibid.*, 261-62.
[105] *Ibid.*, X, 344 (August 7, 1825).
[106] *Ibid.*, IX, 246, To Henri Gregoire (February 25, 1809). To Fanny Wright he spoke of the possibility of the existence of an African nation in which "habits of industry are established, and the arts practised". *Ibid.*, X, 344 (August 7, 1825).

went further than saying that evidence might prove his original observations incorrect. This much he had admitted in the *Notes*. Furthermore, even if Jefferson could have been convinced that he erred
regarding the Negro's aptitude, it is unlikely that his distaste for the
color of the race could have been easily erased.

Jefferson's views on the Negro had led him to oppose firmly any
physical mixture of the two racial stocks. This, in turn, became one
of the foundations of his emphasis upon the necessity of expatriating
freed Negroes. His insistence on this point was as strong in 1826 as
it had been in 1782. "I consider that [plan] of expatriation to the
governments of the W. I. of their own colour as entirely practicable,
and greatly preferable to the mixture here. To this I have a great
aversion. ..." [107] Jefferson certainly was not alone in finding the
Negro's color a negative characteristic. In 1786 the Reverend James
Madison (not to be confused with the statesman of the same name)
wrote to Jefferson of the "Poor Black". "It seems as if Nature had
absolutely denied to him the possibility of ever acquiring the com-
plexion of the Whites." [108]

A clearer perspective on the depth, bias and intellectual respec-
tability of Jefferson's ideas on the Negro can best be obtained by
comparing them with those of men whose names have been linked
with his as devotees of the Enlightenment: fellow members of the
American Philosophical Society and especially the Virginia Dynasty
he dominated. Benjamin Rush, whom history can more readily desig-
nate an avowed abolitionist than an able physician, felt that the
Negro was degraded by his unfortunate color and features. However,
Rush's science held great prospects for the future of that race. According to the doctor, the thick lips, flat nose, black color, and wooly
hair, typical of the Negro, were actually symptoms of leprosy, a
disease which Rush claimed to have more than once observed. Also
attributed to leprosy by Rush was the relative insensibility of the
Negro's nerves and his ability to endure pain and intense heat. The
leper, like the Negro, Rush observed, was prone to veneral diseases.
He reasoned that the durability of the Negro's color was due to the
fact that leprosy was, of all diseases, the most permanently inherited.
He declared that, since the disease had ceased to be infectious, all
that remained was to seek its cure. Rush was certain that a cure would
lead to the collapse of such arguments as that the black color had

[107]   *Ibid.*, 362, To William Short (January 18, 1826).
[108]   Boyd, *Papers of Jefferson*, X, 643 (December 28, 1786).

marked the Negroes as objects of God's wrath, or that the pigmentation of their skin had destined or qualified them for labor in hot and unwholesome climates. Rush felt these beliefs were basic to slavery's rationale; once removed, the institution would be dealt a crushing blow.[109]

In addition to opposing slavery, Rush shared Jefferson's belief that the Negroes themselves preferred the color of the whites, and he also felt the races should remain apart as long as the difference remained.[110] However, Rush's science, unlike Jefferson's, offered vigorous support for his anti-slavery arguments. It envisioned a day when a common color would erase the basic distinction between master and slave and make unnecessary elaborate plans for expatriation and colonization. He did not share Jefferson's fears of racial amalgamation. On the contrary, he stated:

It is possible, the strength of intellects may be improved in their original conformation, as much as the strength of the body, by certain mixtures of persons of different nations, habits, and constitutions, in marriage. The mulatto has been remarked, in all countries, to exceed in sagacity his white and black parent. The same remark has been made of the offspring of the European and North American Indian.[111]

Other American scientist-humanitarians refused to admit color as an acceptable excuse for treating one man differently from another. David Rittenhouse addressed inhabitants of other planets:

... you are perhaps more happy still, that all communication with us is denied. We have neither corrupted you with our vices nor injured you by violence. None of your sons and daughters degraded from their native dignity, have been doomed to endless slavery by us in America merely because *their* bodies may be disposed to reflect or absorb the rays of light, in a way different from ours.[112]

Benjamin Barton, in his *Elements of Botany*, referred to the incongruity between the beauty and symmetry of the rice plant and the ugliness of the social order which enslaved the Negroes who cultivated it.[113]

[109] Daniel J. Boorstin, *The Lost World of Thomas Jefferson* (New York, Henry Holt and Co., 1948), 90-91, citing *Transcripts of the American Philosophical Society*, IV, 283 ff.: Read to Society (July 14, 1792).
[110] *Ibid.*, 92.
[111] Benjamin Rush, *Sixteen Introductory Lectures* (Philadelphia, 1811), cited by Boorstin, *The Lost World of Thomas Jefferson*, 268.
[112] Rittenhouse, *Orations*, 19, cited by Boorstin, *The Lost World of Thomas Jefferson*, 196.
[113] Page 29, Volume II, of Barton's work cited in Boorstin, *The Lost World of Thomas Jefferson*, 196-97.

Perhaps no individual has been as closely associated with Jefferson's political career as James Madison. In his will, Jefferson spoke of the "cordial and affectionate friendship which for nearly now an half century has united us in the same principles and pursuits of what we have deemed for the greatest good of our country".[114] Madison had introduced in the Virginia legislature the slavery bills of the Revisors; Jefferson had confided in him and sought his assistance relative to the publishing of the *Notes*; Jefferson also expressed to Madison his disappointment at the failure of the anti-slavery clause in the Ordinance of 1784. However, these instances appear to have constituted the extent of their exchanges on the issue of slavery. There is no evidence among the published works of further discussions on any aspect of the problem.

Madison's dislike for slavery appears to have been as intense as Jefferson's. He had entered upon a career in law in order to avoid the life of a planter, and gain a livelihood depending "as little as possible upon the labours of slaves".[115] Unlike Jefferson, he was willing to see the liberation of the blacks and the enlistment of their aid against the British during the Revolution. He felt such action would be "consonant to the principles of liberty which ought never to be lost sight of in a contest for liberty".[116]

Not only did Madison find the existence of slavery incompatible with the struggle for liberty, but also with the existence of a democratic republic. In the Philadelphia Convention he opposed the twenty year period of grace for the slave trade on the grounds that such a long term would be "dishonorable to the national character". He also thought it improper to "admit in the Constitution the idea that there could be property in human beings".[117]

Madison's approach to the problem in the early years of the nation was quite different from Jefferson's. He neither initiated legislation nor devised schemes for the eventual emancipation of the slaves. His attacks on slavery were less direct. Primarily concerned with the

---

[114] Ford, *Works*, X, 395 (March, 1826).
[115] Gaillard Hunt (ed.), *The Writings of James Madison*, II, 154, cited by Gaillard Hunt, *The Life of James Madison* (New York, Doubleday, Page and Co., 1902), 70.
[116] Hunt, *Writings of Madison*, I, 106, To Joseph Jones (November 28, 1780), cited by Hunt, *Life of Madison*, 70-71.
[117] Farrand, *Records of the Federal Convention*, II, 415-17, cited by Edward McNall Burns, *James Madison, Philosopher of the Constitution* (New Brunswick, Rutgers University Press, 1938), 76.

establishment of an independent, stable republic, he attacked legislative attempts to foster slavery's growth and welfare as not conducive to these aims. Madison appears to have considered the Revolution in predominantly military and legal terms. Far more the lawyer and far less the scientist-humanitarian than Jefferson, there is no indication that Madison viewed the events of the time in the same broad humanitarian terms as did his friend. Perhaps Madison's most eloquent attack on slavery is to be found in a half finished essay entitled, "The Influence of Domestic Slavery on Government." He argued not in defense of humanity and morality, but rather in an area more familiar to him, on the grounds of efficient government. Slavery, he argued, fostered an aristocracy which threatened the existing democratic institutions.[118]

Jefferson had put forth his plans for emancipation and had displayed his greatest optimism during a period in which he felt the spirit of enlightened humanitarianism would sweep the evil away. Madison's interest in more direct solutions of the slavery problem came years later, to a large extent coinciding with Jefferson's period of deepest pessimism. The difference in timing can most probably be attributed to differences in motivation. Madison seemingly awoke to the full extent of the danger of slavery when its great threat to the nation's existence first became blatantly obvious in 1819. His three-fifths compromise might have sufficed in 1783 when men looked at the problem with calmer emotions, but the situation had changed.[119]

Madison's plan for emancipation was offered in a letter to Robert J. Evans in 1819. There is much in it to remind one of Jefferson's proposals, which Madison had earlier endorsed, and it is likely that he was influenced to some extent by them. The basic concept of emancipation followed by expatriation was present. However, the plan had so many loopholes and was so impractical that one can only imagine that the emergency of the Missouri crisis fostered haste rather than careful thought on Madison's part. He proposed that sufficient acreage of the lands belonging to the federal government should be sold over a period of years to provide income for the gradual purchase of slaves from their masters. Since the Constitution

[118]   Department of State, MSS., cited by Hunt, *Life of Madison*, 75.
[119]   This early version of the three-fifths compromise accepted by the Continental Congress served as a model for the similar rule adopted by the Constitutional Convention in 1787; Irving Brant, *James Madison, The Nationalist, 1780-1787* (Indianapolis, The Bobbs-Merrill Company, 1948), 241.

clearly gave no authority to Congress to appropriate money for such purchases, Madison probably envisioned the necessity for an amendment, the passage of which, it would seem, would have been quite impossible in the face of certain Northern and Western opposition. Continuing, Madison proposed that the Negroes thus redeemed from bondage would be transported to a colony to be established in Africa. Certain exceptions would be allowed. Negroes who preferred to remain in slavery rather than face the uncertainty of life in a strange environment would be permitted to do so. Slaves who had been disabled or worn out in the service of their masters would remain a charge upon their former owners. Another exception, which it seems would have, in effect, negated the entire purpose of the scheme, stated that servants whom their masters regarded as too valuable to be disposed of at the price fixed by due process of law would not need to be sold.[120]

Madison expressed an attitude similar to Jefferson's on the Missouri question, stating that the uncontrolled dispersion of slaves would be desirable. He reasoned that the fewer the number of slaves in proportion to the rest of the population in a given area, the better the prospects for improved conditions and for emancipation.[121] Like Jefferson, his enthusiasm for diffusion appears to have been limited to the period of the crisis.

Despite Nat Turner's revolt, the growth of the abolition movement and the failure of attempts at emancipation in the Virginia Convention, Madison's last years were filled with optimism, in contrast to Jefferson. He placed great faith in the American Colonization Society and in 1833 was rewarded by its members with the office of President.[122] Madison's will left the organization two thousand dollars.[123]

The third member of the Virginia triumvirate, James Monroe, might very well be considered a member of what Thomas Jefferson spoke of as "the rising generation" in which he had at first placed such great hopes for eliminating the Negro problem. Governor Monroe, as we have seen, sought and valued the advice of his former

[120] Hunt, *Writings of Madison*, VIII, 437-39, cited by Burns, *Madison*, 77-78.
[121] Hunt, *Writings of Madison*, IX, 25, To James Monroe, cited by Burns, *Madison*, 78.
[122] Although he did not accept the honor, he had earlier given the organization his blessings and expressed confidence in the success of its endeavors; Congress Edition, *Works*, IV, 213, To R. R. Gurley (December 28, 1831), cited by Hunt, *Life of Madison*, 369.
[123] Hunt, *Writings*, IX, 550, cited by Burns, *Madison*, 78.

teacher regarding the treatment of criminal Negroes. However, he does not seem to have ever equalled Jefferson's concern over the Negro problem. Arthur Styron, Monroe's biographer, stated that "he took slavery for granted as a sort of metaphysical evil like war or the prison system." [124]

Of the three Virginia Presidents, only Monroe expressed satisfaction with the Missouri Compromise. He told Jefferson that the contest, so far as the Northern leaders were concerned, had been for power only and that they had been willing — may even have intended — to dismember the Union. He thought that the Compromise was "auspicious" because it would give passions on both sides time to subside and because, in such a controversy, it would have been dangerous for either side to come off victorious.[125]

Of course Monroe's situation at this time was quite different from that of Jefferson and Madison. He was President, obligated above all to serve and maintain the Union. In a letter written on February 15, 1820, he proclaimed his intention of lending his support to any decision which Congress might reach on the Missouri question. If the Constitution permitted limitations upon slavery's expansion, he expressed a willingness to abide by such action.[126]

Perhaps the best reason for Monroe's apparent failure to involve himself in the long range problems of slavery was the fact that he himself was rather removed from the institution. Jefferson and Madison were trained lawyers who had immersed themselves in their responsibilities as planters. Monroe was trained as a lawyer and remained primarily a lawyer all his life. Whereas the two former expressed yearnings to return to their plantation homes when the

[124] Arthur Styron, *The Last of the Cocked Hats: James Monroe and The Virginia Dynasty* (Norman, Oklahoma, The University of Oklahoma Press, 1945), 360.
[125] S. M. Hamilton (ed.), *The Writings of James Monroe*, IV, 122-23 (May, 1820), cited by George Dangerfield, *The Era of Good Feelings* (London, Methreen and Co., Ltd., 1953), 229.
[126] Daniel C. Gilman, *James Monroe* (Boston, Houghton, Mifflin and Company, 1899), 246. The author refers to these views as being contained in a "private letter", but fails to submit further documentation. Having doubts as to the constitutionality of the limitations placed upon slavery's expansion by the compromise bill, Monroe submitted the question to his Cabinet. That body unanimously agreed that Congress had the power to prohibit slavery in the Territories. So that all would be able to answer that the act was constitutional, Monroe had withdrawn a question relative to the situation which would exist after statehood was achieved. The President signed the bill on March 6, 1820; W. P. Cresson, *James Monroe* (Chapel Hill, The University of North Carolina Press, 1946), 348-49.

duties of public office drew to a close, Monroe, as late as 1804, longed to establish a law practice in Richmond.[127] After retiring from the Presidency he spent much of his time in his wife's home town, New York, where he died on July 4, 1831.[128]

Rush, Rittenhouse, Barton, Madison, and Monroe have all been classified as Jeffersonians. They and Jefferson himself shared an outlook on man as a creature of dignity and on government as man's servant. But as there were differences in their personalities and circumstances, there were bound to be differences in their approaches to the Negro problem. The Jeffersonians were noted for supporting their moral science with the data of natural history. The abolitionist-scientist Rush provided an excellent example of such an approach in his discussion of the Negro. Jefferson, in the spirit of nationalism, had produced scientific evidence to refute Buffon's claims of the inferiority of natural American species. Yet, when it came to discussing the racial characteristics of the Negro, he proclaimed his determination to follow wherever the facts might lead. Daniel Boorstin noted this phenomenon and stated, "We may find an irony and perhaps a moral in noting that where the Jeffersonian remained truest to his professed reliance on the facts of natural history was where the ethical faith was least secure." [129]

Thomas Jefferson was probably no less a humanitarian than Benjamin Rush. However, Jefferson was, unlike the good doctor, also a Virginia planter and a Virginia politician. His view of the Negro was, therefore, a complex one. The humanitarian demanded freedom for the Negro as a human being and for the sake of the morals of his master; the planter saw the Negro as an important economic unit, who, in his servile condition, displayed a notable lack of talents; the politician saw in the Negro a threat of physical harm to his constituents in the form of a rebellious slave and later a political danger in the hands of those who wished to use him to obtain political advantage.

The problem of the Negro involved more than questions of morals and science. There were important economic, political and social factors inherent in the slavery question, and Jefferson was well aware of and influenced by them. Throughout his writings on this subject

[127] S. L. Gouverneur, MSS., To Judge Jones (May 16, 1804), cited by Gilman, *Monroe*, 97-98.
[128] Cresson, *James Monroe*, 493-94, 498.
[129] Boorstin, *The Lost World of Thomas Jefferson*, 98.

there are examples of fears which produced doubts and, in turn, doubts which produced fears. When the moment seemed most auspicious, when the moral climate and economic situation appeared to signal the possibility of political action to end slavery, Jefferson devised a plan and waited for the enlightened youth of the state to accomplish the work. However, even at this moment, the scientist in him, conditioned by his slave-holding experiences, expressed doubts of the Negro's capacities and a fear of racial amalgamation. These fears and doubts never left him, but, to his great credit, neither did the belief that the Negro should and must some day be freed.

CHAPTER IV

THOMAS JEFFERSON AND THE INDIAN

Thomas Jefferson's initial contact with the Indian came when he was a young boy. Numerous tribes occupied the Virginia frontier, and at least one of their chiefs often made it a practise to visit Shadwell on his journies to Williamsburg.[1] At college the student Jefferson was given the opportunity of meeting Indian youths brought to William and Mary to imbibe the teaching of Christianity and the ways of white man's civilization. In 1812 Jefferson wrote to John Adams of his early experiences with red men. "I was very familiar with the Indians, and acquired impressions of attachment and commiseration for them which have never been obliterated. Before the revolution, they were in the habit of coming often and in great numbers to the seat of government, where I was very much with them."[2]

As a youth Jefferson was particularly taken with the Cherokee Chief Outassete. This Indian obviously provided him with one of the most impressive and lasting experiences of his life. The occasion was vividly recalled by Jeffeson at least forty-three years later:

I was in his camp when he made his great farewell oration to his people the evening before his departure for England. The moon was in full splendor, and to her he seemed to address himself in his prayers for his own safety on the voyage, and that of his people during his absence; his sounding voice, distinct articulation, animated action, and the solemn silence of his people at their several fires filled me with awe and veneration, although I did not understand a word he uttered.[3]

---

[1] The Cherokee Outassete appears to have taken advantage of Peter Jefferson's hospitality on numerous occasions. Ford, *Works*, IX, 358, To John Adams (June 11, 1812). Jefferson's biographer John Dos Passos gives the impression that other chiefs also visited Shadwell; John Dos Passos, *The Head and Heart of Thomas Jefferson* (Garden City, New York, Doubleday and Co., Inc., 1954), 232.
[2] Ford, *Works*, IX, 358 (June 11, 1812).
[3] *Ibid.*, To John Adams (June 11, 1812).

The "attachments", "commiseration", "awe", and "veneration" which the young Jefferson had felt for at least one Indian helped lay the groundwork for a later interest in numerous scientific and humanitarian projects. Among these were several attempts to determine Indian origins primarily through a study of vocabularies, an evaluation of their capacities as a race, and efforts to derive a plan which would save them from extinction at the hands of an expanding white civilization.

Jefferson's first discourse upon the subject of Indian origin and the character of the race was contained in the *Notes on the State of Virginia*. On the question of origin he supported the possibility of either European or Asiatic roots. However, he gave the impression of leaning toward the latter. "... the resemblance between the Indians of America and the eastern inhabitants of Asia would induce us to conjecture that the former are descendants of the latter, or the latter of the former." [4]

Jefferson declared in his *Notes* that the best road to determining Indian derivation would be through a study of "their several languages".[5] Shortly afterwards he commenced a compilation of Indian vocabularies, which he continued in hopes of eventual publication until his entire collection was stolen from his saddle bag sometime between 1806 and 1809.[6] Despite this misfortune, his fascination with the subject continued to the last years of his life. In the very last letter concerned with Indians to be found in his published writings, Jefferson thanked his correspondent for sending him a Cherokee vocabulary and commented on the multiplicity and variances of American Indian languages.[7]

Jefferson's interest and enthusiasm had mounted as his vocabularies grew. From such sources as Benjamin Hawkins, the Indian agent, and James Madison, he received keys to different tribal languages.[8] The world traveler John Ledyard must have spurred Jeffer-

[4] *Ibid.*, III, 205.
[5] *Ibid.*, 206-7.
[6] Jefferson's first written report of the theft was in a letter to Dr. Barton on September 21, 1809; Bergh, *Writings of Jefferson*, XII, 312-13. The last reference to his active collecting was made on April 18, 1806, in a letter to Leverett Harris; *ibid.*, XI, 102-3.
[7] *Ibid.*, XVI, 107-9, To . . . . [sic] (February 20, 1825).
[8] Boyd, *The Papers of Jefferson*, IX, 640, From Benjamin Hawkins (June 14, 1786). Hawkins sent vocabularies of the Cherokees. *Ibid.*, XIV, 436, To James Madison (January 12, 1789). Jefferson thanked Madison for sending him a Mohican vocabulary.

son to further investigate the relationship between the languages of
Asia and those of the American Indians. Through the medium of
numerous letters, Ledyard took Jefferson around the world and enabled him to partake of the mysteries of the less frequented areas
of the globe. From a spot described as the "Town of Barnowl in
Siberia", Ledyard, on July 29, 1787, penned a most interesting letter,
filled with the enthusiasm of a man who believed he had made a
great discovery:

I shall never be able without seeing you in person and perhaps not even
then to inform you how universally and circumstantially the Tartars resem-
ble the aborigines of America. They are the same people—the most ancient,
and most numerous of any other, and had not a small sea divided them,
they would all have still been known by the same name. The cloak of
civilization sits as ill upon them as our American tartars. They have been
a long time Tartars and it will be a long time before they are any other
kind of people.[9]

Jefferson recognized Ledyard as a "person of ingenuity and information, who, upon arriving safely home, could provide new, various,
and useful information." However, believing that Ledyard also had
"too much imagination", he continued to rely most heavily upon the
more scientific approach of comparative linguistics.[10]

On April 18, 1806, Jefferson wrote a letter to Leverett Harris on
the subject of Indian origin. His words reflected his pride in accomplishment. He told Harris that he had made such great progress in
gathering the vocabularies that in a year or two he would offer them
for publication. He asked Harris to obtain for him a copy of Pallas'
Vocabulaires compares des langues de toute la terre, in which were
included seventy-three Asiatic words common to his Indian vocabulary. Jefferson hoped that this work would enable him "to make the
inquiry so long desired, as to the probability of a common origin
between the people of color of the two continents".[11]

This letter is the last reference to the vocabularies to be found
among Jefferson's writings until September 21, 1809, when he wrote
to Dr. Barton telling of the theft of his valued collection.[12] With the
theft his active participation in the search appears to have come to

[9]   *Ibid.,* XI, 638.
[10]   This estimate of Ledyard was contained in a letter to Charles Thompson;
ibid., XII, 160 (September 20, 1787).
[11]   Bergh, *Writings of Jefferson,* XI, 102-3.
[12]   *Ibid.,* XII, 312-13.

an end. In 1813 he told John Adams, "... the question of Indian origin, like many others, pushed to a certain height must receive the same answer, 'Ignoro'."[13] The only expressed conclusions based on his studies of the various languages are found in a letter to Dr. Peter Wilson, Professor of Languages, Columbia College, dated January 20, 1816:

... I can, from memory, say nothing particular, but that I am certain more than half of them differed as radically each from every other, as the Greek, the Latin, and Icelandic, and even those which seemed to the derived from the same radix, the departure was such that the tribes speaking them could not probably understand one another. Single words, or two or three together, might perhaps be understood, but not a whole sentence of any extent or construction.[14]

Given far more attention in his *Notes* than the question of origin was that of the Indian's racial capacities. Count de Buffon had declared that the natives of South America, like all of nature's species found in America, were inferior to those of Europe. Jefferson dismissed these statements as "fables" as reliable as those of "Aesop". Since he was far more familiar with the Indians of North America and placed greater faith on the "truth and judgement" of those who had written of them, Jefferson utilized his knowledge of those Indians to answer the Frenchman's allegations.[15]

Beginning with emotional characteristics, Jefferson took issue with Buffon's representation of the Indian as having less ardor and being more impotent than the white. He emphasized the Indian's bravery, consideration and affection for children, loyalty to friends, keen sensibility, "vivacity and activity of mind". In all these characteristics but one Jefferson stressed their similarity to the whites. Only in writing of the Indian's bravery did he describe an exceptional trait, but in a manner not at all detrimental to the race:

... he is brave, when an enterprise depends on bravery; education with him making the point of honor consist in the destruction of an enemy by strategem, and in the preservation of his own person free from injury; or perhaps, that is nature, while it is education which teaches us to honor force more than finesse. ... [16]

Jefferson acknowledged that the drudgery to which Indian women

13 *Ibid.,* XIII, 248 (May 27, 1813).
14 *Ibid.,* XIV, 402.
15 Ford, *Works,* III, 151.
16 *Ibid.,* 151-52.

were submitted was unjust, but insisted that this was the case with every barbarous people. "Were we equal in barbarism, our females would be equal drudges." Turning to the realm of physical characteristics, Jefferson stated that the comparative weaknesses of their men and strength of their women was easily explained. ". . . our man and their woman is habituated to labor; and formed by it. With both races the sex which is indulged with ease is the least athletic." [17]

The fact that Indian women produced fewer children than their white counterparts, Jefferson argued, was due not to differences in nature, but in circumstances. Having to accompany their men in hunting and war activities, childbearing was an inconvenience which they avoided, often by procuring abortions. He pointed out that the squaws of white traders produced and raised as many children as white women.[18]

Jefferson stated that claims that the Indians have less hair than the whites, except on the head, were without proof. He explained that the Indians plucked their hair as fast as it appeared, considering a hairy individual to be like a hog. As evidence, he again turned to the squaws of white traders. Furthermore, he denied the entire concept which stated that the amount of hair on the body was directly related to the degree of an individual's ardor, declaring that the "Negroes have notoriously less hair than the whites; yet they are more ardent." [19]

Jefferson also found it necessary to defend the Indians against charges that they were mentally inferior:

Were we to compare them in their present state with the Europeans North of the Alps, when Roman arms and arts first crossed these mountains, the comparison would be unequal, because, at that time, those parts of Europe were swarming with numbers, because numbers produce emulations and multiply the chances of improvement, and one improvement begets another. Yet I may safely ask, how many good poets, how many able mathematicians, how many great inventors in arts and sciences, had Europe, North of the Alps, then produced? And it was sixteen centuries after this before a Newton could be formed.[20]

Turning on Buffon, he questioned the reasoning which stated on one hand that the cold and moisture of the New World reduced the physical stature of the races of animals, and on the other hand ad-

[17]   *Ibid.*, 153-54.
[18]   *Ibid.*
[19]   *Ibid.*, 154-55.
[20]   *Ibid.*, 159-61.

mitted that the physical stature of the Indian was generally equal
to that of the European:

How has this 'combination of the elements and other physical causes, so
contrary to the enlargement of animal nature in this new world, these
obstacles to the development and formation of great terms' been arrested
and suspended, so as to permit the human body to acquire its just
dimensions, and by what inconceivable process has their action been
directed on his mind alone.[21]

Jefferson felt that, although further study was necessary, it would
probably be shown that the Indians were "formed in mind as well as
body, on the same module with the 'Homo sapiens Europeans'".[22]
He readily admitted belief in the existence of varieties in the races
of man, distinguished by their powers of body and mind, but he took
issue with thought suggesting that these were dependent to some
extent on which side of the Atlantic the species existed. "Whether
nature has enlisted herself as a Cis- or Trans-Atlantic partisan? I am
induced to suspect there has been more eloquence than sound
reasoning displayed in support of this theory...."[23]

In 1785, the year his *Notes* first appeared in print, Jefferson again
referred to the subject of Indian capacities in a lengthy letter to
Chastellux. He stated that the only respectable evidence of Indian
inferiority had been offered by Don Ulloa. Abbe Raynal, Robertson,
Buffon, and DePauw, he pointed out, had based their charges on
secondary sources of information. Don Ulloa's testimony was to be
respected because he wrote of what he saw. Jefferson hastened to
add, however, that Ulloa observed the Indian from an unfortunate
vantage point. His South American Indians "had passed through ten
generations of slavery," and Jefferson felt it "very unfair, from this
sample, to judge the natural genius of this race of men".[24]

Jefferson insisted that such a picture was no indication of what
their ancestors were like three hundred years earlier. Only in North
America were the Indians observable in their original character, and
here, he stated, they were on a level with whites in the same uncultivated state. Jefferson told Chastellux of having seen "some
thousands" of the race and having received "much information" from
those who had lived among them. Pointing to the results of these

[21]   *Ibid.*, 155.
[22]   *Ibid.*
[23]   *Ibid.*, 162-66.
[24]   Boyd, *Papers of Jefferson*, VIII, 185 (June 7, 1785).

investigations as evidence, he proclaimed, without any reservations whatsoever, that he believed "the Indian then to be in body and mind equal to the whiteman".[25]

It is difficult to avoid surmising that Jefferson's statements on this subject were conditioned by the spirit of nationalism as well as the letter of science. Unlike the section of his *Notes* dealing with the Negro, he was engaged to a large extent in "Query XI" in answering and refuting charges by Europeans which reflected negatively on the products of the American hemisphere. Immediately after dealing with Buffon's allegations, he turned on Abbe Raynal, who extended the doctrine of inferiority to apply to the race of whites transported from Europe.[26]

One cannot help noticing that, while Jefferson was insistent that the condition of slavery stifled the Indians and that any attempt to evaluate their natural attributes from such a position was unfair, he had proclaimed, in the case of the Negro, that slavery offered all sorts of advantages for the advancement of the race.[27]

To deny that Jefferson's arrival at fixed opinions and his scientific observation could have been influenced by factors other than pure reason would be to make of him something more than human. His reaction to Indian oratory had been largely emotional. The very appearance of the Indian must have bespoken a harmony with the whites. In writing of his distaste for the Negro's appearance, Jefferson had revealed a preference for a fine mixture of red and white, flowing hair and symmetry of features.[28] To such an eye the Indian probably was not unattractive.

Whether it was youthful emotion, scientific curiosity, or a combination of both which triggered it, Jefferson's interest in the Indian was intense and far ranging. In addition to speculating about Indian origin and racial characteristics, his "Query XI" contained a detailed description of the tribes of Virginia, their governments, numbers and their burial grounds. The latter he had personally investigated through diggings.[29] In his discussion of Virginia's educational establishments, contained in "Query XV", Jefferson offered the suggestion that the Indian School at William and Mary, known as the Brafferton Institution, would have its purposes better served by utilizing its funds

25   *Ibid.*, 185-86.
26   Ford, *Works.*, 167-68.
27   *Ibid.*, 245-46.
28   *Ibid.*, 244.
29   *Ibid.*, 195-96, 198-204.

to maintain a perpetual mission among the Indians. Thus, in addition to instructing them in the principles of Christianity, as required by the founder, information could be gathered regarding their traditions, laws, customs, languages, "and other circumstances which might lead to a discovery of their relations with one another, or descent from other nations".[30]

It is not surprising that Jefferson placed little value on the primarily religious emphasis of the Indians' training at Williamsburg. In later years he stated that "to begin" with religious education "has ever ended either in effecting nothing or in grafting bigotry on ignorance".[31]

Jefferson's views on the racial characteristics of the Indian appear to have been supported in large measure by his colleagues of the American Philosophical Society. They found the Indian's copper skin so much like the white man's as to suggest nothing more than a difference of variety.[32] Samuel Stanhope Smith, Benjamin Rush and Benjamin Barton all produced arguments to prove that the intellectual inferiority of Indians was really a mask placed on them by their environment which, when removed, would show them to be equal in all respects to the white man.[33]

The Philosophical Society showed an avid interest in discovering objects which could lend support to an equalitarian argument and instructed its permanent committee to obtain plans of ancient fortifications, tumuli, and other objects of art. When Barton examined remains from the Northwest, he rejoiced at their testimony to the essential talents of the Indians, which confirmed "the relation of man to God; and the relations of men to each other".[34]

While Jefferson shared the interest in antiquities, he felt that some of his companions in the Society were too hasty in arriving at conclusions based upon their scattered findings. He wished travellers to the Northwest "would make very exact descriptions of what they see ... without forming any theories. ... We must wait with patience

---

[30] *Ibid.*, 256. Jefferson had included these suggestions in his Bill No. 80, "A Bill for Amending the Constitution of the College of William and Mary ...", Boyd, *Papers of Jefferson*, II, 543.

[31] Bergh, *Writings of Jefferson*, XI, 395, To James Pemberton (November 16, 1807).

[32] Boorstin, *The Lost World of Thomas Jefferson*, 85. Author cites, as an example, Benjamin Rush's statement that the Indian's color was produced by environment (*Introductory Lectures*, 166 f.).

[33] *Ibid.*, 85-86.

[34] *Ibid.*, 87-88, citing *Transactions of the A. P. S.*, IV, 187 ff.

till more facts are collected." [35] It appears that Jefferson felt that the systematic study of Indian vocabularies was a superior method of determining their origin and relationship to other peoples of the globe.[36]

During the Revolutionary War, Jefferson delivered an address to a visiting Indian chief, Jean Baptiste Ducoigne, who had offered his tribe's support in fighting the British. The chief was advised that, unless they had suffered injury at the hands of the Red Coats, the best course for his people's welfare would be to remain neutral. Jefferson spoke of a wish to see the Indians multiply and be strong and promised to fulfill their request for schoolmasters. "We desire, above all things, to instruct you in whatever we know ourselves. We wish to learn you all our arts and to make you wise and wealthy." [37] Commenting upon this address, Julian Boyd states:

... it sets forth most of the sympathetic and farsighted views on the status and future of the Indian that were to be embodied in T. J.'s Indian policy as President.

That T. J. at this critical moment and in the very last hours of his governorship took the trouble to show the Kaskaskia chief every honor and to give him sound and sincere advice is a measure of his feelings for the Indians as a race.[38]

William T. Hagan, in his work *American Indians*, gives his readers a rather different view of Jefferson's approach to the race. He states that, despite Jefferson's "frequently proclaimed devotion to human rights", he "was not color blind when the inevitable conflict between settlers and Indians arose". Hagan describes Jefferson's Indian policy as suggesting "the sort of duplicity Hamilton saw in his personality".[39]

Undoubtedly supporters of either interpretation would have little difficulty finding evidence among Jefferson's words and deeds to

[35] Boyd, *Papers of Jefferson*, XII, 159, To Charles Thomson (September 20, 1787).
[36] The Philosophical Society also recognized the value of collecting vocabularies and, in 1799, listed among the principal duties of its permanent committee the inquiry into the languages of the American Indian; Boorstin, *The Lost World of Thomas Jefferson*, 79.
[37] Boyd, *Papers of Jefferson*, VI, 61-63, Speech to Jean Baptiste Ducoigne (June, 1781).
[38] *Ibid.*, 63 n.
[39] William T. Hagan, *American Indians* (Chicago, The University of Chicago Press, 1961), 53-54.

buttress their position. To arrive at the key to this dilemma, it is necessary to examine what he said and did, and what circumstances were involved at the time of the statements and deeds. It is also necessary to keep in mind the complexity of this man who was at the same time a politician, scientist and humanitarian.

The Indian presented a somewhat different problem to Jefferson as a public servant than did the Negro. For the most part, the majority of the latter race, in a state of slavery, posed no immediate threat to the white populace. It was primarily in the cases of freed Negroes and the slave trade that Jefferson was obligated to formulate policies for their control; therefore, much of his concern and plans regarding slavery were expressed in the future tense. The Indians presented a different picture. Jefferson did not have to convince anyone that the presence of this savage, hunter race on the frontier represented a real danger to lives, property and future plans for the westward expansion of white civilization. As Governor of Virginia, Secretary of State, and President, he was called upon to share in and bear responsibility for the formulation and execution of Indian policy. Decisions were required in times of peace and in times of war to treat with Indians as allies, enemies and neutrals.

The aforementioned speech to Jean Baptiste was made in the closing hours of the Revolutionary War. The sentiments voiced contrast markedly with those of the early days of the conflict, when the Indian represented a threat or at least a possible hindrance to the war efforts of the Virginians. Regarding tribes which had allied themselves with the King's cause and attacked Virginian communities, Jefferson wrote in 1776, "Nothing will reduce these wretches so soon as pushing the war into the heart of their country. But I would not stop there. I would never cease persuing [sic] them while one of them remained on this side of the Mississippi." [40]

As for enlisting Indians to be used against the enemy, he termed them a "useless, expensive, ungovernable ally".[41] To tribes that appeared to be contemplating war against the Americans, he echoed the statements of the Continental Congress, which made it quite clear that, for the sake of their very existence, they had better maintain neutrality. The Six Nations had been warned "that if they did not take the most decisive measures for the preservation of neutrality,

[40] Boyd, *Papers of Jefferson*, I, 485, To John Page (August 5, 1776). Reference is to the Cherokees.
[41] *Ibid.*, 500, To John Page (August 20, 1776).

we would never cease waging war with them while one was to be found on the face of the earth".[42]

Jefferson's policy for dealing with hostile Indians was clearly stated time and again in his letters to George Rogers Clark. Clark had been directed by the Virginia Legislature to carry the war into Indian territory in order to "revenge" the past injuries committed by the Indians and "punish" the agressors. On January 3, 1778, Jefferson told Clark that his soldiers, who would soon be victorious at Kaskaskia, were each to receive three hundred acres of conquered Indian land as a gift from the Burgesses.[43] A year later Jefferson suggested to Clark a choice of summer campaigns, either against the Indians situated between the Ohio and Illinois Rivers or against British held Detroit. "If against these Indians, the end proposal should be their extermination or their removal beyond the lakes or the Illinois river." [44]

As Governor, Jefferson was by no means consistent in urging a policy of neutrality among uncommitted Indian tribes. In the Western campaign he completely disregarded such sentiments. He told Clark:

Endeavor that those who are in friendship with us live in peace also with one another. Against those who are our enemies let loose the friendly tribes. The Kikapous should be encouraged against the hostile tribes of Chickasaws and Choctaus and the others against the Shawnese.[45]

For those Indians who allied themselves with Clark, ammunition was to be supplied "gratis". To encourage others to offer their services, ammunition and skins were to be supplied "with a disposition to do them very friendly office, and to gain their love".[46]

In 1781, though directives for campaigns against the Indians continued to emanate from the Governor's desk, Jefferson appears to have begun to give increased attention to the establishment and maintenance of peaceful relations with the Indians. This was the year of the speech to the Indian chief, Jean Baptiste Ducoigne. We also find correspondence with an Indian agent to whom Jefferson wrote of peace and friendship with the Indians as his desire and in their interest. He apologized for his inability to furnish goods for the In-

[42] Bergh, *Writings of Jefferson*, IV, 279, To . . . . . [sic] (August 13, 1776). Bergh states that the letter was probably written to Edmund Pendleton (275 n.).
[43] Boyd, *Papers of Jefferson*, II, 132-33.
[44] *Ibid.*, III, 258-59 (January 1, 1779).
[45] *Ibid.*, 276 (January 29, 1780).
[46] *Ibid.*, 276-77.

dians due to the exigencies of war but promised "as the principal reward for their sufferings, a hearty and cordial friendship with us, with free commerce and plentiful supplies on the restoration of peace".[47]

With the return of peace the nature of Jefferson's references to the Indians underwent a change as striking as the quiet following a summer storm. Relieved of the responsibilities of the governorship, there is no evidence among his published writings of a single mention of Indians for more than a year after the victory at Yorktown. During the years 1783-1790 most of the remarks pertaining to the Indians contained in Jefferson's letters reflected his scientific interest in the red man. Residing in Paris from 1784 to 1789, he undoubtedly received many queries concerning the American Indians. The distance from the frontier also probably encouraged him to focus upon the scientific rather than the political aspects of the problem. It was during these years that Jefferson completed and published his *Notes on the State of Virginia,* initiated his study of Indian vocabularies, and corresponded at great length on the subject of Indian origin with Chastellux, DeMeunier, John Ledyard, Benjamin Hawkins, and others. His proximity to the excesses and intrigues of European governments appears to have encouraged an even greater interest in the Indians, whose life of rustic simplicity seemed to contrast markedly with the extremes he found on the Continent. Comparing Indian society, with its lack of a formal governmental structure, to those of Europe, he wrote in 1787, "Among the former, public opinion is in the place of law, and restrains morals as powerfully as laws ever did anywhere. Among the latter, under pretense of governing, they have divided their nation into two classes, wolves and sheep." [48]

The infrequent allusions to the Indian problem which Jefferson made during these years in Paris reflected primarily his status as a representative of the United States. In 1786 he told DeMeunier that purchases of land from the Indians would be made at distant intervals of time as the settlements slowly pushed westward and "that not a foot of land" would "ever be taken from the Indians without their own consent". He assured the Frenchman that the "sacredness" of the Indians' rights was "felt by all thinking persons in America as in Europe".[49] The same year he informed the Dutchman, Van Hoo-

[47] *Ibid.,* IV, 600, To Linctot (February 13, 1781).
[48] *Ibid.,* XI, 49, To Edward Carrington (January 16, 1787).
[49] *Ibid.,* X, 166 (June 22, 1786), contained in Jefferson's "Observations on De

gendorp, that numerous treaties with the Indians were being undertaken, which would provide salable land, the revenues from which
would quickly absorb the entire domestic debt.[50] Less than two
weeks prior to the letter to Van Hoogendorp, in a communication to
the Indian agent, Benjamin Hawkins, he described the flaunting of
Indian rights as "a principal source of dishonour to the American
character".[51]

The differences of shading in these descriptions of the status of
Indian lands and American attitudes toward their savage neighbors
undoubtedly can be explained by the nature of Jefferson's correspondents. He had devoted numerous pages of script describing to De-
Meunier the glories of things American. He obviously was more
interested in convincing Van Hoogendorp of American solvency than
describing America's savagery. Benjamin Hawkins was a champion
of just treatment for the Indian and certainly would not have been
impressed by allusions to sympathetic views of the Indians held by
"all thinking persons in America". In the letter to Hawkins, Jefferson
included what appears to have been his first exposition upon a
general policy for dealing with the Indian nations:

The two principles on which our conduct toward the Indians should be
founded are justice and fear. After the injuries we have done them, they
cannot love us, which leaves us no alternative but that of fear to keep
them from attacking us. But justice is what we should never loose sight of.
And in time it may recover their esteem.[52]

There is reason to believe that this statement to Hawkins represented,
with some degree of accuracy, Jefferson's personal views at the time.
This is indicated by his frank espousal of the necessity for instilling
fear in the hearts of the Indians in a letter to a man so devoted to
their welfare. Also, it is to be remembered that Jefferson had supported a policy of fear directed at neutral and potential enemy tribes
during the Revolutionary War. As for the primacy of justice in the
two-fold approach, one need not elaborate on Jefferson's numerous
statements supporting the principle.

Though the assertions regarding Indian policy made in Paris are

---

Meunier's Manuscripts". De Meunier was preparing articles on the United States
for the *Encyclopedie Methodique* and asked Jefferson to answer numerous questions pertaining to the subject.
[50] *Ibid.*, 298-99 (August 25, 1786).
[51] *Ibid.*, 240 (August 13, 1786).
[52] *Ibid.*

interesting, the ultimate test of their significance comes when they are compared with statements elsewhere and, more important, the deeds of a Jefferson directly involved with Indian affairs. He became so involved in 1790, upon assuming the office of Secretary of State in Washington's cabinet.

During his tenure as Secretary of State Jefferson's pronouncements on Indian policy generally called for the primacy of the federal government in questions involving Indian lands and trade, and for steps which would insure permanent peace along the frontier. In cases involving land grants in Indian territory by the states of Georgia, North Carolina, South Carolina and Virginia, Jefferson stood firmly by federal authority. His opinion of the Georgia land grants during the early days of the Yazoo imbroglio was typical of this position. He stated that there were two means of acquiring native title. "First, war; for even this may, sometimes, give a just title. Second, contracts or treaty." Now, he declared, both powers were given by the Constitution exclusively to the federal government.[53]

Time and again Jefferson reminded correspondents of the fact that only the national government could treat with the Indians regarding matters of trade and land cession.[54] He was particularly adamant in seeing to it that neither states nor individuals infringed upon Indian territory. In a letter to Henry Knox regarding the activities of the South Carolina Yazoo Company, Jefferson wrote:

I am of the opinion that the Government should firmly maintain this ground; that the Indians have a right to the occupation of their lands independent of the States within whose chartered lines they happen to be, that until they cede them by Treaty or other transaction equivalent to a Treaty, no act of a State can give a right to such Lands, that neither under the present constitution, nor the ancient Confederation, had any State or person the right to Treat with the Indians, without the consent of the General Government . . . and that if any settlements are made on lands not ceded . . . without the previous consent of the United States, the Government will think itself bound, not only to declare to the Indians that such settlements are without the authority or protection of the United States, but to remove them also by the public force.[55]

One who wishes to find in Jefferson's declarations evidence of concern for and good will toward the Indian would have little difficulty. Interspersed here and there are statements such as "the Government

---

[53] *Ibid.*, XVI, 407, "Opinions on Certain Georgia Land Grants" (May 3, 1790).
[54] *Ibid.*, Ford, *Works*, V, 37, 215, 305, 370, 425.
[55] Ford, *Works*, V, 370 (August 10, 1791).

is determined to exert all its energy for the patronage and protection of the rights of the Indians" and "a leading object of our present Government is to guaranty them in their present possession, and to protect their persons with the same fidelity which is extended to its own citizens." [56] However, one may also observe motives which are far less doctrinaire than either a dedication to upholding federal authority or a determination to protect Indian rights. Jefferson was distressed at the expense incurred in pacifying the Indians. Peace appealed to him as an advocate of fiscal soundness as well, and perhaps even more than, as a humanitarian. A multiplicity of agencies and individuals treating with the tribes increased the chances for disagreements which could lead to expensive wars. Here very possibly lay one motivation for his support of federal authority. In 1792 Jefferson wrote:

The U.S. find an Indian war too serious to risk incurring one merely to gratify a few intruders with settlements which are to cost the other inhabitants of the U.S. a thousand times their value in taxes for carrying on the war they produce. I am satisfied it will ever be preferred to send an armed force and make war against the intruders as being more just and less expensive.[57]

War was not entirely disavowed by Jefferson as a method for pacifying the Indians. What he did demand, as he had during the Revolution, was complete victory. A term he often employed was "drub". A letter written to James Monroe in 1791 presents an interesting illustration of his impatience with what he considered to be a lackadaisical military effort in the Northwest. Also quite evident is the emphasis placed upon avoiding a large public debt and his repugnance toward the concept of a standing army:

I hope we shall drub the Indians well this summer and then change our plan from war to bribery. We must do as the Spanish and English do, keep them in peace by liberal and constant presents. They find it the cheapest plan, and so shall we. The expense of this summer expedition would have served for presents for half a century. In this way, hostilities being suspended for some length of time, a real affection may succeed on our frontiers to that hatred now existing there. Another powerful motive is that in this way we may leave no pretext for raising or continuing an army.

[56]   Ibid., To Henry Knox (August 10, 1791); Bergh, Writings of Jefferson, VIII, 197, To Mr. Dumas (May 13, 1791).
[57]   Ford, Works, V, 489, To David Campbell (March 27, 1792).

Every rag of an Indian depredation will otherwise serve as a ground to raise troops with those who think a standing army and a public debt necessary for the happiness of the U.S. and we shall never be permitted to get rid of either.[58]

Again in 1793 Jefferson raised his voice to demand a strong stand against the Northwest Indians. When the Cabinet met to discuss, for the sake of peace, the propriety of returning to the Indians land which they had previously ceded, Jefferson issued the lone objection. He was only willing to offer the Indians a promise to withhold from settlement those lands in the vicinity of tribal territory.[59] When efforts at a treaty with these Indians were inaugurated, Jefferson expressed a lack of confidence in the possibility of their success and, later, annoyance at the delay they caused in initiating full scale military operations.[60]

Despite expressions of interest in the rights and welfare of the Indians, it appears that Jefferson's conception of an Indian policy was dictated essentially by concern for the nation he served. During these years as Secretary of State he spoke of peace primarily in terms of the benefits which would accrue to the white man. The goal was clear and precise — pacification of the Indians. The means of obtaining and maintaining it varied. The aggressive policy he advocated to subdue the Northwest tribes contrasted noticeably with his plans for dealing with the Indians of the South. Regarding the latter hostiles, he appears to have supported the policy of avoiding the use of governmental force. More subtle means were used to attempt to remove the Indians from the war path. The running of the boundary line with the Creeks was suspended and the United States commissioners in Spain were instructed to inform that government of our displeasure at its incitement of the Indians.[61] When the occasion appeared opportune, Jefferson supported more devious attempts to arrive at a solution. Such was the case when, on June 1, 1793, the Cabinet suggested:

[58] *Ibid.*, 319 (April 17, 1791).
[59] *Ibid.*, VI, 191, "Cabinet Opinion on Indian War" (February 22, 1793).
[60] *Ibid.*, 300, To U.S. Minister to France (June 13, 1793); Bergh, *Writings of Jefferson*, IX, 258, To Thomas Pinckney (November 27, 1793); Ford, *Works*, VI, 462, To Dr. Enoch Edwards (December 30, 1793).
[61] Bergh, *Writings of Jeffeson*, VIII, 425-26, To Carmichael and Short (November 3, 1792). Also, Ford, *Works*, VI, 118 (October 14, 1792), and VI, 231 (May 31, 1793). Jefferson accused the Spanish of inciting the Creeks, Choctaws, Chickasaws, and Cherokees.

That an agent be sent to the Choctaw nation to endeavor secretly to engage them to support the Chickasaws in their present war with the Creeks—giving them, for that purpose, arms and ammunition sufficient; and that it be kept in view, that if we settle our differences amicably with the Creeks, we at the same time mediate effectually the peace of the Chickasaws and Choctaws; so as to rescue the former from the difficulties in which they are engaged, and the latter from those into which we may have been instrumental in engaging them.[62]

Perhaps one reason for the avoidance of direct action with the Creeks was suggested in a letter which Jefferson wrote less than two weeks after the Cabinet plotted the above strategy. In the letter he emphasized the strength of the Creeks and the great distance which separated them from areas heavily populated with whites.[63] It is also possible that Jefferson felt that pressure brought to bear upon the Spanish foreign office regarding their incitement of the Indians would be more effective than similar action directed at powerful Britain. After acknowledging, on February 2, 1792, a British disclaimer of Canadian support and encouragement of Indian hostilities, there is no record among Jefferson's published works of his broaching the issue until the summer of 1793, when he subtly advised the British minister that, "Were the Western posts in our possession, it cannot be doubted but there would be an end to the murders daily committed by the Indians on our North Western frontier." [64]

The years during which Jefferson served as Governor of Virginia and Secretary of State were marked by almost continuous clashes between the whites and Indians along the Western and Southern frontiers. His Indian policies do not appear to have differed remarkably from what one can imagine would have been those of any other able man in his position. His treatment of Indians as wards, allies, and enemies never seems to have extended beyond what was in the best immediate interests of his constituents. It is quite likely that Jefferson did not relish this type of contact with the red men. It was not as an enemy that his initial interest in the race had been aroused. But as Jefferson stated in 1791, when discussing his relationship to Indians as both a student of natural history and a public servant, "The first is my passion, the last is my duty. . . ." [65]

[62] Ford, *Works*, VI, 275-76. This opinion appears to have been unanimous.
[63] *Ibid.*, 300, To the United States Minister to France (June 13, 1793).
[64] *Ibid.*, V, 436, To the British Minister (George Hammond) (February 2, 1792); *ibid.*, VI, 321, draft of a letter to Hammond (June 20, 1793).
[65] *Ibid.*, V, 294, To Harry Innes (March 7, 1791).

There is no record of a single reference to the Indian as a political problem among the published collected writings of Jefferson from 1794 until his First Annual Message in 1801. Perhaps this may be partially explained by the relative quiet along the frontier during these years, but it also appears likely that, once relieved of policy making responsibilities, he gladly shifted his attention to the collecting of Indian vocabularies. During the winter of 1793-1794 the punitive actions of the Tennessee settlers had proven much more effective than the diplomacy of the Washington administration in subduing the Southwestern Indians, and 1794 and 1795 saw Wayne's victory at Fallen Timbers and the Treaty of Greenville bring peace to the Northwest. Yet it appears that Jefferson, who had been so immediately involved in these problems, offered no comment upon their outcomes. A letter to Benjamin Hawkins in 1800 indicates the direction which Jefferson's interest took during these years. He told the Indian agent that he had reached the stage in his collection and study of vocabularies where publication was iminent.[66]

Unlike the case of the Negro, Jefferson had not included in the *Notes on the State of Virginia* a detailed plan for the solution of the Indian problem. Apparently his initial public statement along these lines came in his First Annual Message, when he announced his belief that an agricultural way of life was best for the Indians, as well as the whites. He told Congress:

Among our Indian neighbors ... a spirit of peace and friendship generally prevails; and I am happy to inform you that the continued efforts to introduce among them the implements and the practise of husbandry, and of the household arts, have not been without success; that they are becoming more and more sensible to the superiority of this dependence for clothing and subsistence over the precarious resources of hunting and fishing; and already we are able to announce that, instead of constant diminuation of their numbers, produced by their wars and their wants, some of them begin to experience an increase in population.[67]

Jefferson continued to preach the desirability of the agricultural way of life for the Indian throughout his administration. To Indian chiefs and their white friends he spoke of a bounteous future for the red men. He told them that hunting had already become an insufficient means of furnishing clothing and subsistence. The promotion of agriculture and household manufacturing was essential to their existence,

[66] *Ibid.*, VII, 436 (March 14, 1800).
[67] *Ibid.*, VIII, 113-14 (December 8, 1801).

and he promised to aid and encourage these endeavors. The removal of the Indian need for vast acres of land would fit the demands for more territory by the expanding white population and thus remove the great source of contention between the races. He told Benjamin Hawkins:

In truth the ultimate point of rest and happiness for them is to let our settlements and theirs meet and blend together, to intermix, and become one people. Incorporating themselves with us as natural citizens of the United States, this is what the natural progress of things will of course bring on, and it will be better to promote than retard it.[68]

During Jefferson's first two years in office his Indian policies reflected to a large degree his earlier views on the race. Though the principles of maintaining peace, acquiring lands and civilizing the Indians had been standard during the administrations of Washington and Adams, there were important differences of emphasis in the policies and methods of Jefferson. The defeat of the Indians in the Northwest enabled him to rely more upon the traditional methods of diplomacy and less upon military measures. In 1802 Congress approved Jefferson's request that the Act of 1796 establishing and maintaining trading factories be revived.[69] The same year, also at Jefferson's request, Congress provided that $15,000 per year be employed in efforts to civilize the Indians.[70] During most of the first two years, with the exception of the Georgia tribes, the Indians were not pressed to cede lands. Rather attempts were made to secure confirmation of pre-Revolution Indian cessions of Great Britain and France and to mark the boundaries between white and Indian lands.[71] Jefferson appears to have been willing to wait until the transformation to agriculture produced a willingness on the part of the Indians to give up their former hunting grounds.

During this period, Jefferson also displayed an understanding and

[68] *Ibid.*, 213-15 (February 18, 1803). These sentiments are repeated over and over again in the various addresses made to Indians by Jefferson from 1801 to 1809; Bergh, *Writings of Jefferson*, XVI, 370-472.
[69] Richard Alton Erney, "The Public Life of Henry Dearborn", unpublished Ph. D. thesis, Teachers College, Columbia University, 1957, 95, citing Act of 30 April, 1802, *Annals* 7th Congress, 1st session, 1348.
[70] *Ibid.*, 123, citing Harmon, *Sixty Years of Indian Affairs*, 158-59.
[71] In April, 1802, Georgia finally ceded her western lands to the United States, on condition that the federal government clear the Indian title to all lands still included within the state boundaries; Erney, "Dearborn", 92, 256, citing Articles of Agreement between Georgia and the United States (April 24, 1802), Carter, *Terr. Papers,* V, 142-46.

respect for the Indian way of thinking and concern for their physical health. On January 28, 1802, in the course of a special message to Congress, he recommended that the law regarding crimes committed by Indians, which in certain cases required the punishment of death by hanging, be changed to call for military execution, "the former way being peculiarly repugnant to their ideas". In the same address, he urged the prohibition of the sale of alcoholic beverages to Indians.[72]

On December 29, 1802, two weeks after he delivered his Second Annual Message, Jefferson penned a lengthy discourse entitled "Hints on the Subject of Indian Boundaries". Rumors of possible French reoccupation of Louisiana undoubtedly led him to declare, "An object, becoming one of great importance, is the establishment of a strong front on our western boundary, the Mississippi, securing us on that side, as our front on the Atlantic does toward the East." He called for the rapid purchase of Indian lands along the Mississippi. Hemmed in between the Atlantic barrier on the East and the Mississippi on the West, the Indians would thus be forced to turn to agriculture. Though he wrote of the benefits of agriculture and of just treatment for the Indians, the tone of the message indicates the establishment of a policy of manipulating the Indians in such a way that their interests would serve and be secondary to those of the nation. During most of the first two years of his administration Jefferson had spoken of the Indians in collective terms and had inaugurated a general policy. Now he listed the various Mississippi River tribes individually and suggested individual prescriptions to hasten their removal. Speaking of the strategically located Chickasaws, he stated, "What we know in favor of the other Indians should not constitute the measures of what we do for these, our views as to these being so much more important."[73]

The trading factories which had been established were to be used now to aid directly in obtaining Indian land. Jefferson urged that the Chickasaw chiefs, who were particularly hesitant about ceding land, be encouraged to run into debt at these factories "beyond their individual means of paying, and whenever in that situation, they will always cede lands to rid themselves of debt."[74]

On January 18, 1803, Jefferson sent a confidential message to

[72] Bergh, *Writings of Jefferson*, III, 349-50.
[73] *Ibid.*, 373-74.
[74] *Ibid.*

Congress in which he urged the continuance of the act for establishing trading factories and outlined his plan for a buffer of white settlements along the Mississippi. While speaking of the agricultural way of life as being in the best interest of the Indian, he made it quite clear that this aspect of Indian policy was also an important factor in the nation's military posture. At this time he also broached the question of a possible expedition to explore the Missouri River "even to the western ocean", the main incentive being that the river "and the Indians inhabiting it, are not as well known as is rendered desirable by their connection with the Mississippi, and consequently with us".[75]

That civilization through agriculture had, by 1803, become the handmaiden for Jefferson's policy of obtaining Indian land without war is made strikingly clear in three letters written early in that year. He told Andrew Jackson flatly that the agents among the Indians had two objectives, the preservation of peace and the obtaining of lands, and stated, "Toward effecting the latter object we consider the leading of the Indians to agriculture as the principal means from which we can expect much effect in the future." [76]

Jefferson also told Jackson that, as far as he could see, charges that agent Benjamin Hawkins was more attached to the interests of the Indians than those of the United States were based upon suspicion rather than proof. Jefferson declared that "toward the preservation of peace" Hawkins was "omnipotent", and "in the encouragement of agriculture" he was "indefatigable and successful". However, he assured Jackson that, if proof were made available that showed Hawkins to have obstructed Indian cessions, he would be "placed under as strong a pressure from the executive to obtain cessions as he could from any opposite quarter to obstruct". Jackson was informed that Hawkins would be made sensible of the fact that his value would be estimated in proportion to the benefits he could obtain for the nation.[77]

Perhaps to set the record straight, two days after penning his letter to Jackson, Jefferson wrote to Benjamin Hawkins to, as he told the Indian agent, inform him of his "personal dispositions and opinions" on the Indians. Devoting most of the letter to explaining to this champion of Indian rights the great advantage which would accrue

[75] *Ibid.*, 489-93.
[76] *Ibid.*, X, 357-58 (February 16, 1803).
[77] *Ibid.*, 358-59.

to the red men upon abandoning the hunter's way and adopting agriculture, Jefferson finally got to the point:

It is possible, perhaps probable, that this idea of agriculture leading to citizenship and amalgamation with the whites may be so novel as that it might shock the Indians, were it even hinted to them. Of course, you will keep it for your own reflection; but convinced of its soundness, I feel it consistent with pure morality to lead them towards it, to familiarize them to that idea that it is for their interest to cede lands at times to the United States, and for us to procure gratification to our citizens, from time to time, by new acquisition of land.[78]

Jefferson then told him of pressure from Georgia to obtain Creek land and urged him to attempt to persuade the Creeks to cede.[79]

Attempting to get his western barrier policy moving in the north, Jefferson wrote to William Henry Harrison on February 27, 1803. The ratio between the length of his dissertation on the desirability of agriculture for the Indians and the discussion of the need for securing our western boundary was quite the reverse of that in the letter to Hawkins. Evidently having no reason to doubt Harrison's attachment to the primacy of national interest, Jefferson was far more frank and to the point, so much so that he urged Harrison to regard the contents as highly secret.[80]

It is interesting to note the views and suggestions in this letter which were not included in the one to Hawkins. For one thing, Jefferson specified the policy of getting the chiefs into debt to facilitate land cessions. Though speaking of eventual incorporation with the whites as citizens as being the "most happy" future outcome for the Indians, he told Harrison that, if this were not possible, they would have to be removed to lands west of the Mississippi. Another double edged sword to be used in dealing with the Indians was "love" and "fear". Jefferson emphasized the need "to cultivate their love". However, he also stated, "Should any tribe be foolhardy enough to take up the hatchet at any time, the seizing the whole country of that tribe, and driving them across the Mississippi, as the only condition of peace, would be an example to others, and a furtherance to our federal consolidation."[81]

Jefferson urged Harrison not to reveal to the Indians the long

[78] Ford, *Works*, VIII, 213-15 (February 18, 1803).
[79] *Ibid.*, 215.
[80] Bergh, *Writings of Jefferson*, X, 369-73.
[81] *Ibid.*, 370-71.

range aspects of his policy. "For their interests and their tranquility it is best they should see only the present age of their history." He suggested that, when dealing for cessions with one tribe, the minds of the others "should be soothed and conciliated by liberalities and sincere assurances of friendship". However Harrison was given free rein in accomplishing his mission and urged to press forward rapidly:

Of the means ... of obtaining what we wish, you will be the best judge; and I have given you this view of the system which we suppose will best promote the interests of the Indians and ourselves, and finally consolidate our whole country to one nation only. .... The crisis is pressing; whatever can now be obtained must be obtained quickly. The occupation of New Orleans, hourly expected, by the French, is already felt like a light breeze by the Indians. You know the sentiments they entertain of that nation; under the hope of their protection they will immediately stiffen against cessions of lands to us. We had better, therefore, do at once what can now be done.[82]

In these hours when national security appeared threatened, Jefferson reverted to an attitude toward the Indians reminiscent of that displayed during the Revolution — neutralize the Indians by peaceful means if possible, but, if necessary, completely subdue them. Even the concept of physical removal beyond the point of danger was an echo of earlier declarations.

It is clearly observable in Jefferson's letters and messages that, with the acquisition of Louisiana in the autumn of 1803, the sense of urgency and haste regarding the acquisition of Indian lands diminished. Whereas in his Second Annual Message he had discussed Indian affairs in terms of land cession, in his Third and Fourth Messages he again returned to the importance of the agricultural way of life and increased commerce with the Indians for ensuring harmony between the races.[83] In his Second Inaugural Address, going beyond the subject of pacifying the Indians, Jefferson offered the most extensive public airing thus far of his long range hopes for civilizing them. Again speaking of the Indians with sympathy and in general terms, Jefferson declared:

The aboriginal inhabitants of these countries I have regarded with the Commiseration their history inspires. Endowed with the faculties and the

[82]   *Ibid.*, 372-73.
[83]   Ford, *Works*, VIII, 183, "Second Annual Message" (December 15, 1802); *ibid.*, 269-70, "Third Annual Message" (October 17, 1803); *ibid.*, 329, "Fourth Annual Message" (November 8, 1804).

rights of men, breathing and ardent love of liberty and independence, and occupying a country which left them no desire but to be undisturbed, the stream of overflowing population from other regions directed itself on these shores. . . .[84]

Having reaffirmed his faith in the capacities of the Indian and his adherence to the concept of the "rights of men", Jefferson outlined his plan to allow the people whose misfortunes, he reminded his audience, were no fault of their own, to "maintain their place in existence". He called for a continuance of the supplies of men and material to aid them in developing the agricultural and domestic skills, which he referred to as "the acts of first necessity". Such a course, he maintained, would "prepare them in time for that state of society, which to bodily comfort adds the improvement of mind and morals".[85]

One cannot help but note that the image of the red man presented in this address was quite different from that drawn in time of war. Rather than the unscrupulous savage warrior, we have here the displaced child of nature, threatened with extinction by a civilization incompatible with his own and also by what Jefferson referred to as "anti-philosophers" amongst the Indians "who . . . exert all their faculties to maintain the ascendency of habit over the duty of improving our reason and obeying its mandate".[86]

Jefferson's Fifth and Sixth Annual Messages presented to Congress a glowing picture of the great advances made by "our Indian neighbors" and their growing affection for the white man. In the fifth address, as well as the fourth and third, Jefferson also informed the legislators of numerous acquisition of Indian territory. The Kaskaskias, Delawares, Piankeshaws, Chickasaws, Cherokees and Creeks were listed as being among those who had ceded portions of their land.[87]

From the position of these announcements in his speeches, the reader is led to believe that Jefferson meant to imply that the lands were acquired as the fruits of the hunter-to-farmer policy. However,

[84] *Ibid.*, 344, "Second Inaugural Address" (March 4, 1805).
[85] *Ibid.*, 344-45.
[86] *Ibid.*, 345. Jefferson apparently was aware of the activities of the Prophet among the Indians.
[87] *Ibid.*, 269-70, "Third Annual Message" (October 17, 1803); *ibid.*, 329, "Fourth Annual Message" (November 8, 1804); *ibid.*, 394, Draft of "Fifth Annual Message" (December 3, 1805); *ibid.*, 491, "Sixth Annual Message" (December 2, 1806).

he was always prepared to employ other methods of acquiring land. In 1803 when he learned that the Choctaws were considering a sale of land to the British trading concern of Panton, Leslie and Company, to whom they were heavily indebted, he took the position that the government could not allow British subjects to own lands within the United States. However, he was willing that the federal government obtain the land and in turn meet the Indian obligations. Since the Chickasaws were especially reluctant to cede their lands, the President suggested in 1804, that "personal advantages" be offered to their principal men. Credit to the chiefs at the trading factory might influence them.[88]

The fact of the matter is that Jefferson's "Mississippi barrier" policy appears to have remained in effect even after the immediate cause for its inception had been removed with the purchase of Louisiana. William Henry Harrison, who had been given a free hand by the President, was able to report that by January, 1805, sixty million acres of land had been acquired from the Northwest tribes for an average price of one-fourth of a cent per acre.[89] These tribes, among which Tecumseh and the Prophet were to have their greatest success, were not known to take readily to agricultural pursuits.

In 1807 when the activities of the two brothers, as well as the British navy, produced a war scare, Jefferson, recognizing the major source of Indian discontent, told his Secretary of War Henry Dearborn:

... We ought absolutely to stop our negotiations for land, otherwise the Indians will think these preparations are meant to intimidate them into a sale of their lands, an idea which would be most pernicious and would poison all our professions of friendship to them. The immediate acquisitions of the land is of less consequence to us than their friendship and a thorough confidence in our justice. We had better let the purchase lie till they are in a better temper.[90]

When Jefferson first suggested this course of action in August, he obviously felt it would be a temporary expedient, for he initially thought of the Prophet as being a scoundrel who only needed his price.[91] However, upon learning of the activities of the Governor of

[88] Erney, "Dearborn", p. 118, citing *Jefferson Papers*, Library of Congress, Jefferson to Dearborn (January 22, 1803 and October 20, 1804).
[89] *Ibid.*, 115, citing *Jefferson Papers*, Library of Congress, Dearborn to Jefferson (January 12, 1805).
[90] Bergh, *Writings of Jefferson*, XI, 354 (September 2, 1807).
[91] *Ibid.*, 325, To Henry Dearborn (August 12, 1807).

Upper Canada among the tribes, he concluded that what he thought was a "transient enthusiasm" represented a potentially explosive situation.[92]

The news of British activity in the Northwest caused Chief Jefferson to again apply the war paint. He ordered Dearborn to instruct Governors Hull and Harrison to urge the Indians to pursue a course of neutrality in any future conflict between Great Britain and the United States. The Indians were to be reminded of the paternal policy pursued toward them by the United States and assured of the government's peaceful intentions. However, it was to be made clear, as Jefferson stated, "... if ever we are constrained to lift the hatchet against any tribe we will never lay it down till the tribe is exterminated, or driven beyond the Mississippi." [93]

Jefferson also offered the question, as a subject for consideration, whether, upon satisfactory evidence that any tribe contemplated attacking, it might not be better to strike first, before matters between Britain and the United States reached the point where the Indians might expect aid from the Red Coats. Dearborn was told to instruct his agents to discriminate among the tribes in bringing them the President's message, "softening them to some, and strengthening them to others".[94]

Jefferson proceeded with caution, particularly in the Northwest, in dealing with the Indians during the latter part of 1807 through 1809. He admitted being unsure of the motives of the Prophet. Perhaps he wasn't an antiphilosopher after all but "endeavoring to reform the morality of the Indians, and encourage them in industry and peace ...". If this was the case, Jefferson proclaimed himself prepared to do what he could to aid the Prophet's endeavors and "to render his influence as extensive as possible".[95]

Jefferson appears to have been convinced that, if his long range plans for the Indians were to succeed in the Northwest, greater progress would have to be made in the encouragement of agriculture, and the Americans would have to replace the British in winning Indian affection. In his Seventh Annual Message on October 27, 1807, he pointed out that the contrast between the peaceful conditions

[92] Ford, *Works*, IX, 131-32, To Henry Dearborn (August 28, 1807).
[93] *Ibid.*, 132-33.
[94] *Ibid.*
[95] Bergh, *Writings of Jefferson*, XII, 37-38, To Colonel William A. Washington (April 24, 1808). It is interesting that among the published writings of Jefferson there is not a single reference to Tecumseh.

among the Southern tribes and the potentially dangerous situation in the Northwest was attributed to the former's progress in the development of agriculture and the household arts.[96]

In a letter to the Quaker missionary James Pemberton, Jefferson explained that the introduction of agriculture among the Indians of the South had been facilitated by their ability to raise cotton and from the plant weave cloth to replace the hides previously obtained on the hunt. Climate, he pointed out, prevented the Northern tribes from following suit, and the great abundance of wolves made sheep raising impractical. Jefferson suggested that the Indians make the destruction of these beasts one of the principal objects of their hunts.[97] Writing to Dearborn of an offer he had received to teach Indian boys in the vicinity of Detroit agriculture and mechanics, and their sisters spinning and weaving, he urged his Secretary of War to consider offering financial assistance to the endeavor.[98]

To check British influence among the Indians, Jefferson stressed the importance of obtaining control of their commerce and of demonstrating examples of justice, interest in their welfare, and respect for their customs. To John Jacob Astor, he wrote, on April 13, 1808:

> I learn with great satisfaction the disposition of our merchants to form into companies for undertaking the Indian trade within our own territories. . . . You may be assured that in order to get the whole of this business passed into the hands of our own citizens, to oust foreign traders, who so much abuse their privilege by endeavoring to excite the Indians to war on us, every reasonable patronage and facility in the power of the Executive will be afforded.[99]

Jefferson communicated his enthusiasm for the Astor venture to Meriwether Lewis, emphasizing to the Governor of Louisiana that "nothing but the exclusive possession of the Indian commerce can secure us their peace".[100] The President commented to Dearborn that the proposed trading factories on the Missouri and Mississippi would have a greater effect upon the Indians than an equal number of

[96]   Ford, *Works,* IX, 159-60.
[97]   Bergh, *Writings of Jefferson,* XI, 394-95 (November 16, 1807). Jefferson does not appear to have acknowledged the possibility that one reason for the differences in the rate of progress might have been the differences in the attitudes of Hawkins and Harrison.
[98]   *Ibid.,* XII, 40 (April 29, 1808).
[99]   *Ibid.,* 28.
[100]   *Ibid.,* 100 (July 17, 1808).

armies and added, "It is on their interests that we must rely for their friendship and not on their fears." [101]

This rejection of the use of fear marks a departure from earlier statements and policy. Just the previous year he had advocated the use of harsh warnings to admonish the Northwestern tribes against thoughts of war. It appears probable that the change was fostered for practical reasons by the immediate circumstances rather than because of any sudden change in basic philosophy. In 1807 Jefferson's position was affected by the belief that war was imminent. In 1808, the immediate danger having abated, he seems to have been concerned about the role the Indians might play in a possible Anglo-American conflict in the future. Brandishing military might in the face of the Indians could well have had the adverse effect of driving them into a military alliance with the British. The activities of the Canadian Governor in 1807 indicate that such a possibility would have been in no way repugnant to the government of George III.

In addition to encouraging trade with the Indians, Jefferson took other steps during the concluding months of his administration to ensure Indian friendship. In the case of four Iowa Indians accused of murdering a white and delivered up to Meriwether Lewis for justice, Jefferson displayed a keen appreciation of the Indian concept of fair play, as well as a realization that white man's justice had always been able to distinguish the features of an Indian, even through her blindfold. Such expression of common sense and understanding are so rare in the history of Indian relations that a large part of his letter merits being quoted. Discussing Lewis's supposition that at least three of the Iowas would be hanged, Jefferson wrote:

As there was but one white murdered by them, I should be averse to the execution of more than one of them, selecting the most guilty and worst character. Nothing but extreme criminality should induce the execution of a second, and nothing beyond that. Beside their idea that Justice allows only man for man, that all beyond that is new aggression which might be expiated by a new sacrifice of an equivalent number of our people, it is our great object to impress them with a firm persuasion that all our disposition towards them are fatherly; that if we take man for man, it is not from a thirst for blood or revenge, but as the smallest measure necessary to correct the evil, and that though all concerned are guilty, and have forfeited their lives by our usages, we do not wish to spill their blood as long as there can be a hope of their future conduct. We may make a merit of restoring the others to their friends and their nation, and furnish a motive for obtaining a sincere attachment. There is more reason for

[101] *Ibid.*, 140 (August 20, 1808).

this moderation, as we know we cannot punish any murder which shall be committed by us on them. Even if the murderer can be taken, our juries have never yet convicted the murderer of an Indian.[102]

From the President's desk also came orders to remove squatters from tribal lands and pressure to prohibit the sale of alcoholic beverages to Indians.[103]

Jefferson's Eighth Annual Message abounded in expressions of satisfaction over the current state of Indian affairs. He told Congress of the willingness of the Indians on both sides of the Mississippi to turn over to the government disorderly members of their tribes. He appears to have been particularly pleased at the progress being made in agriculture and household manufacturing among the Southern tribes, concluding his remarks with the news that "one of the two great divisions of the Cherokee nation" was considering asking to be made citizens of the United States.[104]

The fact of the matter is that as early as six months prior to this message Jefferson had addressed the chiefs of the Upper Cherokees on the subject of citizenship. The Indians, it seems, were ready to accept the great prize for their success in adapting to white man's ways. The very mention of this request in his Annual Message indicates that Jefferson was greatly pleased. After all, it was a favorable reflection on his endeavors. However, he was not convinced that the time for such a step had yet arrived. He told the Chiefs that he would be glad to welcome them as "brothers instead of our children", but he urged them to carefully consider whether they were ready for such a step, whether they had all accepted as permanent the farmer's way of life. He then put forth a proposal which had been previously associated with military strategy and the use of force, a method suggested during time of war or impending war to eliminate hostile forces permanently from the vicinity of white settlements. He told the chiefs that if some of his people were not ready to settle down, "We will gladly give them land west of the Mississippi, where they can hunt. . . ." [105]

He again broached the subject of westward migration on January 9, 1809, when he addressed a group of deputies from the Cherokee

[102]   *Ibid.*, 147-48 (August 24, 1808). Jefferson had dwelled on the same subject in a letter written to Lewis on August 21, 1808; *ibid.*, 142.
[103]   *Ibid.*, 188, To Albert Gallatin (November 3, 1808); *ibid.*, XII, 223, To . . . . . . [sic] (December 31, 1808).
[104]   Ford, *Works,* IX, 221-22 (November 8, 1808).
[105]   Bergh, *Writings of Jefferson,* XVI, 434-35 (May 4, 1808).

upper and lower towns. He assured them that those who wished to stay would receive "our patronage, our aid, and good neighborhood", and those who wished to go would be assisted.[106]

It is likely that Jefferson realized that no steps toward citizenship, no eventual amalgation of the races could take place as long as there remained among Indians dissident elements, unhappy with their lot as farmers and yearning to return to the freedom of the forests and adventures of the hunt. However, it is also quite possible that another factor may have been involved in the introduction of the Mississippi offer. Though there is no evidence of great pressure from white settlers, perhaps Jefferson had given some thought during these late months of his administration to what reaction might be at the prospect of large numbers of Indian citizens permanently settled close by on fertile land.

It is quite likely that Jefferson left the White House feeling that his Indian policies had been, on the whole, successful. There was peace along the frontier; the agricultural way of life was progressing, particularly among the Cherokees and Creeks, and vast tracts of lands along the eastern shore of the Mississippi had been obtained from the Indians without resorting to war. There was but a hint in the very last year of his administration that Jefferson might have had some second thoughts about how realistic was his plan for permanent incorporation of the Indians among the whites in the face of the latter's insistence for more land and distrust of red men. However, there is no evidence that he expressed such doubts, and, a month after he left office, he reaffirmed his faith in the policy of civilizing the Indians through agriculture and the household arts. In a letter to James Jay he deprecated the importance of instilling Christianity as the first step toward civilization:

Our experience has shown that this must be the last step of the process. The following is what has been successful: 1st, to raise cattle, etc., and thereby acquire a knowledge of the value of property; 2nd, arithmetic, to calculate that value; 3rd, writing, to keep accounting, and here they begin to enclose farms, and the men to labor, the women to spin and weave; 4th, to read "Aesop's Fables" and "Robinson Crusoe" are their first delight. The Creeks and Cherokees are advanced this far, and the Cherokees are now instilling a regular government.[107]

Later in the same year he urged President Madison to continue the

[106] *Ibid.*, 458-59.
[107] *Ibid.*, XII, 270-71 (April 7, 1809).

work of educating the Indians for the new life. Referring specifically to a farm outside of Detroit which had been acquired by the government, he wrote of the endeavors of two French ladies who had utilized the facilities to instruct Indian girls in the practical arts. He suggested that the War Department should furnish the farm and the houses for the use of the school free of charge and add four hundred dollars per year to facilitate the extension of the program to include boys. He concluded the letter with a discourse upon the value of the "civilized arts" in maintaining peace, and also introduced a new twist in his barrier concept, pointing out that the presence of civilized Indians in the environs of Detroit would present an effective check on the strong tribes further west, the Sacs, Foxes, "etc.". All this, Jefferson explained, could be attained at the low cost of the price of one farm and an increase of four hundred dollars in the annual expenditures for these tribes.[108]

As the years passed Jefferson's allusions to the Indian in his writings became few and far between. It appears that only inquiries like those from John Adams and events as earth-shaking as the War of 1812 could stimulate his pen to action. On June 11, 1812, he assured Adams that those Indians who had made such great progress toward civilization, particularly the Cherokees and the Creeks, would not be effectively seduced by the English in the current war. But for the "backward" tribes he had little hope. They would relapse into barbarism. With the national security endangered by these Indians, Jefferson saw only one clear course, the same he had advocated in previous conflicts. ". . . we shall be obliged to drive them with the beasts of the forests into the stony mountains." [109]

As Jefferson was soon to learn, his prophecy was not supported entirely by ensuing events. Not only were the British able to win the support of the less civilized forces of Tecumseh in the North, but many of the advanced tribes of the South, particularly the Creeks, threw in their lot with the foe.

On December 6, 1813, Jefferson penned a letter to Baron Von Humbolt in which he told of the train of abuses suffered by the United States at the hands of the British. In discussing their activities among the Indians, Jefferson not only expressed enmity toward the

[108] *Ibid.,* 334-37 (December 7, 1809).
[109] Ford, *Works,* IX, 358-59.

forces of the Crown, but also bitter disappointment that all his hopes
for the future of the red men had been destroyed:

You know, my friend, the benevolent plan we were pursuing here for the
happiness of the aboriginal inhabitants in our vicinities. . . . They would
have mixed their blood with ours, and been amalgamated and indentified
with us within no distant period of time . . . but the unprincipled policy of
England has defeated all our labors for the salvation of these unfortunate
people.[110]

Jefferson foresaw a bleak future for the Indians, but one he felt was
inevitable in light of their "savage and ruthless warfare". Such behavior would "oblige" the nation "to pursue them to extermination,
or drive them to new seats beyond our reach". The blame for the
eventual "brutalization, if not extermination of this race" was placed
by Jefferson on the shoulders of the English.[111] Perhaps it may be
said that Jefferson was looking for a scapegoat to bear responsibility
for what he had known for years was in store for the Indians. However, the letter to John Adams tends to refute such an assumption.
Jefferson, at that time, appears to have been truly confident that
those tribes which had most successfully adopted civilized ways
would not hearken to British temptations to leave their fields for the
warpath.

Apparently Jefferson referred in writing to government Indian
policy only twice after 1813. In 1818 he indicated strong disapproval
of President Monroe's request that Congress allow him to suspend
the usual treaty procedures in dealing with the Indians and subject
them to federal laws without requiring their consent. Jefferson expressed the belief that such action, if permitted, would be immoral
and would "stain our history". He felt there was absolutely no cause
for this move, when "a little patience and a little money are so rapidly producing their voluntary removal across the Mississippi...".[112]
It is interesting to note that he did not object at all to the latter
phenomenon. Rather it appears that he had become convinced by
this date that removal was the proper policy to pursue.

The second letter is extremely interesting and helpful in placing
Jefferson's concern for the Indian in the proper perspective. It was
addressed to Jedidiah Morse, dated March 6, 1822. Morse had informed him of the formation of a society for the civilization and

[110] *Ibid.*, 431-32.
[111] *Ibid.*
[112] *Ibid.*, X, 115, To Albert Gallatin (November 24, 1818).

improvement of the Indian tribes. The organization was to be made up of the leaders of all branches of the federal government, all officers of the Army and Navy, Governors of the States, Presidents of colleges and all the clergymen of the land. Jefferson, of course, was asked to add his name to the membership roll.[113] While voicing confidence in the integrity of the organization's views, Jefferson was quite firm in refusing to be associated with its formation and activities. He told Morse that:

... this association is unnecessary; that the government is proceeding to the same object under control of the law; that they are competent to it in wisdom, in means, and inclination; that this association, this wheel within a wheel, is more likely to produce collision than aid; and that it is, in its magnitude, of dangerous example; I am bound to say that, as a dutiful citizen, I cannot in conscience become a member of this society. ...[114]

Aroused at what he considered a threat to federal authority, he repeated his views on the matter first to Madison and then to Monroe, informing the President that he was quite willing to have his letter passed among the members of the administration.[115]

It is apparent that Jefferson could not abide any attempts, whether public or private, to solve the Indian problem which at the same time threatened to interfere with what he considered legally constituted authority and procedure. His opposition to the schemes of both Monroe and Morse was based primarily upon concern for the sanctity of law, rather than consideration for the Indians.

Jefferson, even in the late years of his life, maintained interest in the Indian. As late as 1816 he offered warm praise for the freedom of the individual found in Indian society.[116] As late as 1825, though no longer personally engaged in collecting vocabularies, he was obviously still very much fascinated by the subject. "It will be curious to consider how so many languages so radically different have been preserved by such small tribes in coterminous settlements of moderate extent." [117]

Jefferson's feelings for the Indian were reflected in numerous policies. They can be observed in his extension of the trading factory

[113] *Ibid.*, 203.
[114] *Ibid.*, 207.
[115] *Ibid.*, 207 n., To James Madison (February 25, 1822); *ibid.*, 208, To President Monroe (March 19, 1822).
[116] *Ibid.*, 33, To Francis W. Gilmer (June 7, 1816).
[117] Bergh, *Writings of Jefferson*, XVI, 108-9, To . . . . . . [sic] (February 20, 1825).

system; they can be observed in his endeavors to encourage the Indians to give up the hunt, adopt white men's ways and eventually become intermingled with the white race; they can be observed in his attempts to recognize the Indians' concept of justice and to respect their customs. That trading factories were employed at Jefferson's suggestion purposely to drive the chiefs into debt, that respect for customs and justice for the Indians were acknowledged as means of preventing an Anglo-Indian alliance, that the encouragement of agriculture also resulted in the government's obtaining land to satisfy the military and economic needs of the nation are all factors which might lead one to consider that Jefferson was perhaps two-faced in his dealings with the Indians. If the term did not have such a derogatory connotation, it could be considered a valid description of his position. Jefferson's own distinction between his interest in natural science, which he termed his passion, and his occupation as a politician, which he designated as his duty, might very well apply here. It is probable that Jefferson saw as his duty the need for obtaining Indian land, and it was not entirely an imposed duty. Believing in the benefits a nation derived from an agricultural society, it is likely that Jefferson foresaw that an expanding population would require additional soil. The pressure to remove Indians from territory designated as militarily strategic emanated primarily from Jefferson's own policy of establishing a Mississippi barrier. To reconcile this duty with an honest concern for the Indians' welfare was difficult and perhaps an impossible task, but he tried; more than any President before him, he tried.

One historian has concluded that "Jefferson's Indian policy was one vast equivocation, which only the underlying passion for land could reduce to plain form." [118] That he succeeded so brilliantly in his land policy while failing to provide a permanent solution of the Indian problem does not appear from the evidence at hand to have been the result of equivocation, but rather of the attempt to reconcile his passion with his duty, the latter always being considered primary. The truly great failing, which Jefferson must share with the rest of his race, lay in not considering the preservation of the Indian more than an interest or a desire, in not considering it a duty.

There is nothing among Jefferson's collected writings to indicate that he shared his interest and concern for the Indian with his im-

[118]   George Dangerfield, *The Era of Good Feelings* (London, Methuen and Co., 1953), 27.

mediate successors, Madison and Monroe. Though Madison did at one time send him a pamphlet on the Mohican vocabulary, it appears that the action was similar to that of an individual who watches the mail for a stamp which might interest a philatelist friend.[119] This situation is understandable in view of a statement made by Madison's biographer Irving Brant:

The contrast in Madison's childhood between his reliance on Negroes and dread of Indians greatly affected his adult attitude toward these two tributary races. Inclined by nature to sympathy with the downtrodden and ready to recognize rights which were commonly ignored by Americans, he had seen the tomahawk and torch too visibly in his mind's eye to permit him to view the Indian as anything but a savage.[120]

In Madison's inaugural address and his First Annual Message he offered assurances that he would continue the endeavors to bring civilization to the Indians.[121] However, from what can be gathered from his various biographers, it does not appear that he took a great personal interest in the work. Before and after the War of 1812, the references to the Indians in his messages to Congress rarely involved more than one or two lines. While alluding to efforts to civilize the tribes, there is none of the detail or enthusiasm found in Jefferson's addresses. In one particular, Madison altered the Indian policy of his predecessors. In approving of the negotiations which led to the Treaty of Fort Wayne (September 30, 1809), he resumed the policy of land acquisition which Jefferson, for fear of Indian war, had ordered halted. It was this treaty which provided much of the ammunition for Tecumseh's endeavors to unite the Indians in a military alliance against the whites.[122]

During the War of 1812 Madison provided extensive evidence to support Brant's description of his views toward the Indian. It may be argued that statements made during war in the spirit of patriotism

[119] During his years as President, Jefferson submitted drafts of his annual messages and inaugural addresses to Madison for comments on their content, diction and grammar. At no time did Madison offer suggestions relative to Jefferson's statements of Indian policy; Ford, *Works*, VIII, 108 n., 341 n., 266 n., 385 n., 387 n., 483 n., 485 n.; IX, 213 n. - 215 n.
[120] Irving Brant, *James Madison, The Virginia Revolutionist* (Indianapolis and New York, The Bobbs-Merrill Co., 1941), 48.
[121] Richardson, *Messages*, I, 468, 475.
[122] Dangerfield states that Madison gave the negotiations his blessings against his better judgement. He states, "Mr. Madison was in no position to disapprove of land purchases, for he was an inheritor of an Indian policy that was beyond alteration and that he was bound to abet." Dangerfield, *Era of Good Feelings*, 26.

provide poor examples by which to judge an individual's firm convictions. Jefferson himself had spouted venom toward Indian enemies under similar circumstances. However, the differences between the statements of the two men were in the nature of the language employed and the intensity of emotion which, in Madison's case, appears even on the written page. Over and over again Madison referred to the Indians as savages, a term rarely employed by Jefferson. For example, in his second inaugural on March 4, 1813, he spoke of the Indians as being "eager to glut their savage thirst with the blood of the vanquished" and in the Fifth Annual Message, on December 7, 1813, he described the Indians as having a "propensity for war".[123]

If one were to prepare a ledger, and on one side list Jefferson's various attempts to acquire land and the number of times he mentioned civilizing the Indians to Congress and on the other side do the same for Madison, it might very well be possible to strike a balance. However, it appears that there were basic differences which, it is true, the historian rather than the Indian can appreciate, and they were in terms of personal involvement with Indian policy and concern for the future of that unfortunate race.

If Thomas Jefferson directly influenced James Monroe regarding the formulation of Indian policy, it was not apparent in the writings of the former or the activities of the latter as President. The individual who might be pointed to as having the greatest single influence upon Monroe's early pronouncements was Andrew Jackson. Jackson wrote a lengthy letter to the President on March 4, 1817, urging him to abandon the practise of making treaties with the Indians. He argued that they were subjects and as such Congress could legislate for their care and protection, take and dispose of their land at will as well as provide for their eventual civilization.[124] Monroe answered on October 5, 1817:

The view which you have taken of the Indian title to lands in new territory is new but very deserving of attention. . . . A compulsory process seems to be necessary, to break their habits and to civilize them, and there is much cause to believe that it must be resorted to, to preserve them.[125]

On December 2, 1817, he asked Congress to take into consideration "whether other provisions not stipulated by treaties ought to be

[123] Richardson, *Messages,* I, 525, 536.
[124] John Spencer Bassett (ed.), *Correspondence of Andrew Jackson* (Washington, D.C., Carnegie Institute of Washington, 1926-35), II, 279-80.
[125] *Ibid.,* 331.

made" for the sake of advancing the "liberal and humane" policy of the government toward the Indians.[126] Monroe's views of the Indian problem were stated more specifically in his Second Annual Message on November 16, 1818:

Experience has clearly demonstrated that independent savage communities can not long exist within the limits of a civilized population. . . . To civilize them, and even to prevent their extinction, it seems to be indispensible that their independence as communities should cease, and that the control of the United States over them should be complete and undisputed.[127]

By the 1820's it would have virtually been political suicide for a President to speak of Indian affairs in terms of anything short of removal of the tribes to lands beyond the Mississippi. The drive to clear the eastern states of Indians had been gaining momentum since the War of 1812, and the recent activities of Florida based raiders increased the pressure, especially from Georgia. By 1825 Monroe was recommending removal as the only means of saving the Indians from complete destruction. "Experience has clearly demonstrated that in their present state it is impossible to incorporate them, in such masses, in any form whatever, into our system." [128]

It is not surprising that Jefferson did not express views on Indian affairs to his two successors, for he had seen the crumbling of his dream to at the same time satisfy the land hunger of his nation and save the Indian without either removal or destruction. It is to be remembered that, when Jefferson, in 1818, expressed disapproval of Monroe's Indian policy statement, he did not attack the principle of removal, but rather the suggestion to dispense with traditional treaty procedures.

From what can be gathered from their biographers, it does not appear that Madison and Monroe shared Jefferson's deep concern for the Indian. It is probably unlikely, therefore, that if either of them had served as President from 1801 to 1809, there would have been the same commitment to the attempt to civilize the red man and incorporate him into the main stream of American society. However, one may also speculate that, if Jefferson had been in the White House in the twenties, his policies would not have differed consider-

[126] Richardson, *Messages*, II, 16, First Annual Message.
[127] *Ibid.*, 46.
[128] *Ibid.*, 281, To the Senate and the House of Representatives (January 27, 1825).

ably from those of Monroe. All three Virginians, despite the relative differences in their commiseration for the Indian, attempted above all to serve the national interest. This clearly meant the accumulation of tribal lands and the pacification of the Indian warriors. The varying degrees of pressure exerted on the Indians over the years of their administrations appear to have been determined to a great extent by these factors.

What sets Jefferson apart from others is not what he did for the Indians, but what he wished to do.

CHAPTER V

ANDREW JACKSON AND THE NEGRO

In the American mind Andrew Jackson maintains the position of hero extraordinaire. In stories told to school children, in textbook biographical sketches, in romanticized novels, and in mythological motion pictures an image has emerged of Jackson the Indian fighter who introduced the democracy of the frontier to the White House and who firmly established government by the people.

Jackson was indeed a military hero and undoubtedly his name is permanently affixed to the word "democracy". However, Jackson was far more complex than the hero of this popular image. During much of his life he was a soldier, but he was also a plantation owner and an active politician. At various times he practiced law, dabbled in land speculation, storekeeping, and trading in all manner of goods, including slaves. There was much about him to remind one of the rude frontiersman, but one need only read his letters concerning family affairs and plantation management to recognize marks of the Southern aristocrat.[1] Absent from popular legend and ignored to a large extent by historians is Andrew Jackson's relationship with the Negro and the institution of slavery. Yet, in each of his major capacities, as plantation owner, soldier, and politician, Jackson came in contact with that race and that "peculiar institution".

Negro slaves were an important part of Jackson's economic life during those early years when the practise of law provided his primary employment. It appears that a good portion of the revenue from his legal activities was utilized in transactions for slaves as well as land. W. H. Sparks, an acquaintance of Jackson, described the Nashville lawyer as "embarking in many schemes for the accumulation of fortune, not usually resorted to by professional men."[2] In 1790 Jackson

[1] See Richard Hofstadter, *The American Political Tradition* (New York, Alfred A. Knopf, Inc., 1948), Chapter III.
[2] W. H. Sparks, *The Memories of Fifty Years* (Philadelphia, E. Claxton and Co., 1870), 149.

acquired a tract of land near the mouth of Bayou Pierre, in Claribourne
County, Mississippi Territory, and established a small trading store.
Sparks relates that slaves were among the items which his father-in-
law, Abner Green, purchased from Jackson.[3] Included among Jackson's collected writings is a "List of Negroes for A. Jackson", dated
November 8, 1790. The possession of "One Fellow Daniel", "One
Wench Kate", and "three young ones", lends support to Sparks' statements concerning slave trading, for at this time there is no evidence
that Jackson was personally engaged in agriculture.[4]

In 1795 Jackson's land ventures took him to Pennsylvania. Jackson
and Nashville lawyer John Overton were involved in a speculative
enterprise which consisted of buying land claims in Tennessee or
North Carolina and selling them in Philadelphia. Overton suggested
that part of the money derived from the land sales be used to "purchase somewhere in the lower part of the eastern states such Negroes
we might want for Joel Rice", a customer in Tennessee.[5]

Further evidence that Jackson's trading firm bought and sold
Negroes is found in a letter written by Jackson to N. D. Davidson
on August 25, 1804. Jackson informed his correspondent that "a fellow
answering the description you wanted was bought, but I was fearful
he would not suit you as he had once left his master." [6]

The year 1806 marked the beginnings of Jackson's Hermitage and
his change in status from that of trader to that of master. With the
accumulation of plantation land in Tennessee, Alabama, and Mississippi in the years which followed, Jackson's property in slaves grew.[7]
In 1812 a list of Jackson's taxable property included twenty slaves
and six hundred forty acres.[8] His "Black Polls" in 1825 included

---

[3] *Ibid.*, 150. Sparks claimed to have in his possession bills of sale written by
Jackson to Green. The transaction with Green was cited by James Parton, *Life
of Andrew Jackson* (New York, Mason Brothers, 1860), I, 248, 353-54. An order
for one hundred and ninety dollars worth of supplies from a Natchez merchant,
dated March 4, 1790, supports Sparks' statement concerning the opening of the
store; John Spencer Bassett (ed.), *Correspondence of Andrew Jackson* (Washington, D.C., Carnegie Institution of Washington, 1926-35), I, 8.
[4] Bassett, *Correspondence*, I, 8.
[5] *Ibid.*, 13, June 9, 1795.
[6] *Ibid.*, 109.
[7] For a discussion of the acquisition and locations of Jackson's plantations see
Marquis James, *Andrew Jackson, The Border Captain* (Indianapolis, Bobbs-
Merrill Co., 1933), Chapters VII, IX, XVII. Though Halcyon Plantation in
Mississippi was technically the domain of Andrew Jr., numerous letters indicate
that Andrew Sr. bore the brunt of his son's financial mismanagement.
[8] Bassett, *Correspondence*, I, 212 (January 1, 1812), County of Davidson.

eighty-three slaves in all, "Taxable and Not Taxable".[9] In 1842 Jackson wrote that on his two plantations there were "about one hundred and fifty negroes, old, middle aged and young".[10]

Jackson's military and political activities caused him to be absent from his plantations for great periods of time. However, his letters indicated that he always maintained a substantial measure of control over the affairs at home. Like a good soldier, he appreciated the value of staff officers, but he also knew that the ultimate responsibility for the success of a unit rested with the high command. The analogy between the methods of the master of a plantation and the general of an army is easily discernible in Jackson's case. In the military struggle, he had his soldiers; in the drive for economic well-being, his troops were his Negroes.

Unlike each of his Presidential predecessors, Jackson does not appear to have been troubled by slavery or, for that matter, to have ever given serious consideration to the question of the morality of the institution. To Jackson, it appeared to be a matter of practical economics. Just as he deployed troops upon the battlefield, he utilized his slaves in the best possible manner to insure a profitable enterprise. During periods of personal prosperity, particularly between 1819 and 1823, there is evidence that Jackson was eager to obtain more of that type of property.[11] When, in the last years of his life, his financial situation was critical, Jackson offered Negroes for sale in lots as high as fifty-one to pay debts. He also used them to secure mortgages.[12]

If slaveholders are to be categorized as good or bad, Jackson probably belongs among the former group. He was firm, but for the most part, he was also just. He wanted to obtain good crops, but at the same time he wanted to insure that his Negroes were physically and emotionally sound. There is something about Jackson's attitude toward the personnel of his plantation, both free and slave, that at first glance is reminiscent of the patriarchs of the Old Testament. Like a good father, when away from home, he would write to inquire

[9]   *Ibid.*, III, 272 (January 1, 1825).
[10]   *Ibid.*, VI, 138, To Francis P. Blair (February 3, 1842).
[11]   In 1819 Jackson built the mansion at the Hermitage. Various letters regarding slave purchases are found in *ibid.*, II, 412-13; III, 12, 60, 154, 157, 168.
[12]   Large scale sales of slaves began in 1840 and continued until his death in 1845; *ibid.*, VI, 87, 148, 244.

about the health of his "White and Black family".[13] When a slave became ill, he displayed an interest and concern for his progress, always referring to the Negro by name. As an example, on November 25, 1833, President Jackson wrote to his son Andrew Jr.:

I am happy to hear that Adam is mending. with regard to him and Dicks Hanny, I have wrote Sarah. let the advice I have given to be attended to, and both will get well. little hanah has been too long neglected, let the bandage be put on her as directed at once, get Saml, and Dr. Hogg to prepare and place it, and prescribe the liniment and treatment, the leg must be bandaged so that the *hip cannot move,* and her position must be on her back—*attend to this.*[14]

Jackson's relations with his overseers lend support to the picture of a kind yet firm master. When he suspected an overseer had been unnecessarily harsh with the slaves, he would seethe with indignation. The trouble Jackson had with overseer Graves W. Steele provides an excellent example of this and his general approach to the treatment of slaves. The incident involved the death of two slaves, acknowledged by Jackson in a letter to Captain Jack Donelson on June 7, 1829. "I learn old Ned and Jack are both dead, Jack was a fine boy, but if he was well attended, I lament not, he has gone the way of all the earth." [15] Jackson later received the impression that the deaths of these two and a later third were not entirely natural. On July 4th, he wrote to his son that although he had expected "Old Ned" to die from natural causes, he was "fearful the death of Jack and Jim . . . [was] produced by exposure and bad treatment" because the overseer, Steele, "has ruled with a rod of iron". Jackson could not "bear the inhumanity that he has exercised toward my poor Negroes", and ordered Steele's dismissal "unless he changes his conduct".[16]

Later Jackson learned that the slave Jim died by his own hand, and his tone changed. He expressed confidence in Steele, pointing out that the "death of Jim was a mortifying experience to me, and if it had proceeded from cruel treatment of the overseer, he must have been discharged." [17]

This episode revealed Jackson's sympathetic and paternalistic character. However, why had Jim's death been such a "mortifying

[13] *Ibid.,* IV, 85, To Graves W. Steele (November 7, 1829).
[14] *Ibid.,* V, 228.
[15] *Ibid.,* IV, 42.
[16] *Ibid.,* 49.
[17] *Ibid.,* 62, To Andrew Jackson, Jr. (August 19, 1829).

experience" for Jackson? Perhaps he was vexed by the loss of a trusted and experienced slave, a valuable economic unit. Perhaps the idea if inhumane treatment at the hands of Steele was repugnant to his ethical sensibilities. There is also the possibility that Jackson used the word "mortifying" to mean humiliating. The death of a slave on his plantation stemming from ill treatment could possibly have caused President Jackson political embarrassment. Later, when one of his slaves was injured as a result of maltreatment, Jackson ordered the facts stifled. "You may say to Dr. Hogg, that her lament was occasioned by a stroke from Betty, or jumping over a rope, in which her feet became entangled, and she fell." [18]

It is impossible to state definitely which of these factors prompted Jackson's feelings of mortification; perhaps all did. However, after one examines a large number of Jackson's letters regarding his slaves, it becomes clear that his most frequently expressed intention was to get the maximum amount of labor from each Negro, and that all other considerations were either related to or secondary to this goal. Physical punishment was by no means ruled out on his plantation. "Kindness and humanity" were to be employed toward the slaves "so far as their conduct would permit"; however, they were to be held to "strict subordination".[19] Jackson, soldier that he was, could not abide any form of disobedience and insubordination among his plantation "troops".

When cases of slave insubordination involved his wife, Jackson became particularly irate. Mrs. Jackson often had difficulty in handling the servants. In 1814, while her husband was away fighting the Indians and the British, she wrote, "I have been at a greate Deal of trouble with them ... if I live we will own fewer of them for they vex me often and in my situation It is hurteful...." [20] At a later date, she complained that her maid Betty had been "putting on some airs, and been guilty of a great deal of impudence".[21] Jackson provided a solution to the problem in a letter to Andrew J. Donelson. Stating that "it is humiliation to me to resort to this", Jackson ordered that his overseer Mr. Blair "give her fifty lashes" at the "first disobedience or impudence". If Mr. Blair refused to carry out this punishment, Donelson was instructed to "dismiss him and as soon as I get pos-

[18] *Ibid.*, V, 74, To Major William B. Lewis (May 4, 1833).
[19] *Ibid.*, 73.
[20] *Ibid.*, I, 498 (April 7, 1814).
[21] Jackson wrote of his wife's complaints in a letter to Andrew J. Donelson, July 3, 1821; *ibid.*, III, 87.

session I will order a corporal to give it to her publickly. I am determined to cure her." [22] Thus Jackson, while expressing humiliation, could be as severe with an overseer who drew back from physical punishment as with one who was overzealous in performing it. What was the actual misdeed which so annoyed Mrs. Jackson? The maid took in laundry other than that of the Jackson family!

Jackson at times had to deal with runaway slaves. The problem appeared to have been peculiar to his Alabama plantation, perhaps due to the absence of his personal control. Although Jackson once proclaimed, "I hate chains", nevertheless, he employed chaining and selling down the river as methods of instilling fear and obedience in his slaves.[23] As he explained to Egbert Harris, his Alabama manager, ". . . as far as lenience can be extended to those unfortunate creatures, I wish you to do so; subordination must be obtained first, and then good treatment." [24]

Jackson's plantations were studies in black and white in a figurative as well as literal sense. But the figurative colors were rarely distinguishable for the mind's eye to discern clearly. The Negroes were "unfortunate creatures", but subordination had to precede good treatment. Jackson hated chains, but found it necessary to employ them. Dismissal was prescribed for the overseer who was too harsh as well as the overseer who refused to employ the whip. Accompanying the punishment was the declaration of regret; with the humane gesture lurked the spirit of self-interest.

Though apparently recognizing the unhappy status of those "unfortunate people", no thought of changing their lot, no sense of personal guilt appears to have entered the mind of Andrew Jackson. There is no indication that Jackson ever thought of slavery as being just or unjust. The "peculiar institution" was indispensible to the plantation system, and as a planter he realized its importance and utilized it to the utmost. If Jackson was a good master, it was primarily because he endeavored to be a successful planter. Letters in which he displayed concern for the health of the Negroes often simultaneously contained queries about his livestock and cotton.[25] Jackson evidently felt that in the years to come slavery would continue to be vital to the welfare of his plantations. In his will he left

22 *Ibid.*
23 *Ibid.*, 158, To Egbert Harris (April 13, 1822).
24 *Ibid.*
25 *Ibid.*, V, 105, 224-25, 228, 266, 436, 442.

his Negroes to Andrew Jackson Jr., with the exception of certain domestics bequeathed to his daughter-in-law and grandchildren.[26]

Jackson offered his slaves no promise of freedom on earth. However, while on his death bed, he assured them that in Heaven the prospects would be bright. Old Hannah, a slave, described Jackson's last words to his Negroes:

He then turned to us all and said, "I want all to prepare to meet me in Heaven: I have a right to the Tree of Life. My conversation is for you all. Christ has no respect to color. He dwelleth in me and I dwell in him."[27]

This death bed statement is the only reference found in the published works of Jackson in which he spoke of the Negroes' color as a factor involved in their status.

Andrew Jackson's experiences in the management of Negroes extended beyond the boundaries of his plantations and his role as a master of slaves. On September 21, 1814, General Jackson's chief concern was to defeat the British troops threatening New Orleans. From his headquarters in Mobile, Alabama, Jackson addressed the following message "To the Free Coloured Inhabitants of Louisiana":

Through a mistaken policy, my brave fellow Citizens, you have heretofore been deprived of a participation in the Glorious struggle for national rights, in which our Country is engaged. This shall no longer exist. As sons of freedom, you are now called upon to defend our most estimable blessing. As Americans, your country looks with confidence to her adopted Children, for a valorous support, as a partial return for the advantages enjoyed under her mild and equitable government. As fathers, husbands, and Brothers, you are summoned to rally around the standard of the Eagle to defend all which is dear in existence. Your intelligent minds are not to be led away by false representations. Your love of honor would cause you to despise the Man who should attempt to deceive you. I shall not attempt it. In the sincerity of a Soldier, and the language of truth I address you.[28]

Jackson promised "every noble hearted generous brave freeman of colour volunteering to serve during the contest with Great Britain" the same rewards accorded to white soldiers, including salary, clothing allotment, cash, and land bounties. He assured them that "as a distinct, independent Battalion or Regiment, pursuing the path of

[26] *Ibid.*, VI, 221 (June 7, 1843).
[27] *Ibid.*, 415, as told to William G. Terrell in 1880. Terrell described Hannah as a woman of eighty-nine with a remarkably clear memory.
[28] *Ibid.*, II, 58-59.

glory, you will undivided receive the applause, reward, and gratitude of your countrymen".[29]

Two standard works on the history of the American Negro limit their treatment of Andrew Jackson to this address to the free Negroes of Louisiana.[30] The attraction of his words is understandable. That such sentiments should be voiced publicly in New Orleans five decades before the arrival of Ben Butler appears to be rather astounding. The address also seems remarkable coming from someone who bought and sold Negroes and held them in subservience as slaves. However, it should be recognized that on September 21, 1814, Jackson was attired in the bedecked uniform of a soldier and not in the white linen frock of a planter. Jackson insisted in his address that his words represented the "sincerity of a Soldier". However, the weight of evidence indicates that they more accurately reflected the tactical awareness of a commanding officer. He explained to Louisiana's Governor Claiborne that "an activating motive for the address" was to enroll the Negroes into the ranks so that they "may when danger appears be moved to the rear where they will be kept from doing us injury". Jackson expressed a willingness to employ them against the British if "Their pride and merit entitle them to confidence. . . . If not they can be kept from uniting with them." [31] A month after the victory at New Orleans Jackson told James Monroe that there had been "great fears" that the free Negroes might "unite themselves to the enemy on his approach, and become the means of stirring up insurrection among the slaves". To Jackson it was a question of either having "their part of the population in our ranks or . . . in the ranks of the enemy; and my first efforts were therefore exerted to inspire them with attachments to their feelings and prejudices . . .".[32]

If this incident does not place Jackson among the liberal thinkers regarding the Negro race, it does offer evidence of his tenacity and sense of honor. He insisted that the Negroes continue to be armed, even after Governor Claiborne informed him of opposition to the idea among the whites.[33] When one of his pay-masters indicated

[29]   *Ibid.*
[30]   Carter G. Woodson, *The Negro in Our History* (Washington, D.C., The Associated Publishers, Inc., 1941), 200-1; John Hope Franklin, *From Slavery to Freedom* (New York, Alfred A. Knopf, Inc., 1956), 169.
[31]   Bassett, *Correspondence*, II, 88 (October 31, 1814).
[32]   *Ibid.*, 165 (February 13, 1815).
[33]   *Ibid.*, 76-77, From Governor Claiborne (October 17, 1814); *ibid.*, 82 (October 24, 1814).

displeasure over orders to pay colored troops on the same scale as the whites, Jackson wrote him curtly that he was to perform his duties "whether the troops are white, Black or Tea".[34] On at least one occasion the Negro troops rewarded the General for his gesture of confidence in them. Writing to Monroe from his headquarters below New Orleans on December 27, 1814, Jackson stated that the Negro troops had "manifested great bravery" in a recent skirmish.[35]

Psychologists would probably conclude that Jackson understood the workings of men's minds. He obviously had a keen appreciation of the value of men's "feelings and prejudices" and admittedly used them to his own advantage. Like any other weapon, prejudice could be employed by Jackson against an enemy. When utilized against him by others, as in the case of the reluctant paymaster, it could be parried. Jackson followed a similar approach in his dealings with Negroes. As a tool or weapon utilized to achieve economic and military goals, the Negro was employed skillfully and without introspection. Only when the Negro interferred with these goals was he chastized or cast aside. What is surprising and striking about Jackson's employment of prejudice and use of the Negro is that he himself appears to have remained emotionally uninvolved.

The Negro was involved in other encounters between General Jackson and political leaders following the great victory at New Orleans. A bone of contention arose between Governor Claiborne and Jackson over which of the two was responsible for negotiating with the British for the return of contraband slaves as stipulated in the Treaty of Ghent.[36] Later, in 1819, Jackson tangled with William Crawford, a severe critic of his Florida adventure. Jackson had information which linked Crawford with the alleged slave smuggling activities of Georgia's former governor, David B. Mitchell. On September 28, 1819, Jackson, the former slave trader, wrote a "Private" letter to President Monroe proposing an investigation of Crawford's activities so that "an end may be put to such violent outrages of the laws and morality and officers of the Government if concerned in this inhuman and illegal traffic may be dismissed from office and

[34] Jackson MSS., To W. Allen (December 23, 1814), cited by John Spencer Bassett, *The Life of Andrew Jackson* (New York, The Macmillan Co., 1928), 157.
[35] Bassett, *Correspondence*, II, 128.
[36] *Ibid.*, 155, From Governor Claiborne (January 31, 1815); *ibid.*, 157, To Governor Claiborne (February 13, 1815). Jackson's expressed concern was to attend to the "interests of the citizens". He threatened to arrest the governor and legislature if they interferred with what he considered his sphere of responsibility.

legally punished". At the end of the letter came the barb. "I would here remark that the deposition of Genl David Merryweather of Georgia might throw some light on the subject, disclosing the manner and under what circumstances the agency was given to Gov. Mitchell by Wm. H. Crawford then Sec. of War." [37]

In both the Claiborne and Crawford disputes Jackson employed the slavery issue in a way that would be repeated time and again during his later political career. He viewed slavery as a convenient weapon of political warfare for obtaining objectives often quite remote from the Negro.

In the 1820's Jackson, as a political figure of growing significance, commented frequently upon the slavery question. He reacted to the Missouri crisis by scolding the "Eastern interests" whose alleged humanitarian principles shielded a baser desire for "political ascendency and power". The consequences, he believed, would be disastrous: ". . . it will excite those who is the subject of discussion to insurrection and massacre." [38]

Jackson, who condemned "Easterners" for using slavery as a political weapon, employed it himself a year later without hesitation. In letters to John Quincy Adams and John C. Calhoun he urged these statesmen to make haste in arranging the transfer of Florida from Spain so that the "dreaded evil", the "barbarous traffic" in slaves could be halted.[39] There is good reason to suspect that Jackson was primarily concerned with seeing Florida safely annexed to the United States and that he was resorting to the humanitarian approach to promote this end. His repugnance for the slave trade appears to have been limited to the affairs of Florida, and there was no evidence of distaste for the "barbarous traffic" during his earlier days of personal involvement in the slave trade.

Throughout the remainder of his life Jackson continued to follow the pattern displayed relative to the events in Florida and the Missouri crisis, here using the slavery issue and there attacking its use by others. Internal peace and security, preservation of the Union, national expansion, and perhaps his own political ascendency appear to have been among the issues in which Jackson was primarily inter-

[37] *Ibid.*, 434. On February 14, 1818, Jackson, in a letter to Calhoun, had accused Mitchell of being involved in smuggling into the country a large number of Negroes whom he had purchased at Amelia Island; *ibid.*, 354.
[38] *Ibid.*, III, 21, To Andrew J. Donelson (April, 1820).
[39] *Ibid.*, 57, 58, To Secretary Adams (May 1, 1821 and May 21, 1821); *ibid.*, 58, To Secretary Calhoun (May 22, 1821).

ested. Slavery was something which could at times help or hinder these interests, but was certainly to be avoided by his as an issue unto itself.

In 1830 President Jackson found service for the issue when the possibility of territorial expansion again arose. He reminded his chargé d'affaires in Mexico:

Another great inducement for a new territorial arrangement, as the basis for a lasting peace between the two republics, arises from the influence which the population is fast aquiring and which there is some reason to fear on account of the law liberating their slaves is in a state of considerable disaffection.[40]

In 1833 Jackson attacked those who he claimed used the issue of slavery to make political capital, and thus threatened the Union. There were some striking variations on the theme of 1820. This time he defended the East and placed the blame on men primarily from the South, who also happened to be political foes. Now that nullification was "dead", he believed that a "coalition between Calhoun, Clay, Poindexter, and the nullifiers in the South intend to blow up a storm on the subject of the slave question." Jackson insisted that this group was well aware that no anti-slavery plot existed and was attempting to "arouse the southern people on this false tale". He urged that these men be stopped, for they "would do any act to destroy the union, and form a southern confederacy bounded north by the Potomac River".[41]

Perhaps some might see in this letter an attempt by the President to transfer the blame for creating the slavery issue from the shoulders of Eastern political allies to those of Southern opponents. However, it appears that Jackson's fear of Southern attacks on the Union was sincere. First of all, the recipient of these views, Brig. General John Coffee, was one of Jackson's oldest and closest friends and confidants, rather than a fence sitter whom the President was attempting to convince. Secondly, there is evidence that Jackson had received at least one letter from a leading Southerner whose views lend support to such an analysis. A few months prior to the time when the nullification issue reached its critical stage, John Randolph of Roanoke had written to the President in a tone which suggests one Southerner addressing another:

---

[40] *Ibid.*, IV, 129, To Colonel Anthony Butler (March 23, 1830).
[41] *Ibid.*, V, 56, To Brig. General John Coffee (April 9, 1833).

Of your re-election there can be no doubt but it will be to rule over a dis-membered Empire. . . . Let the fools and knaves in the two Houses of Congress disband and then strike at Cuba. It will give vent and profitable employment for all our now burthensome slaves. It will strengthen the great slave holding Interest. We shall have at the least everything south of James River with the naval depot at Norfolk. . . . Nations like men can be governed only by Interest; and the Slave Interest has the knife at its throat in the hands of Fanatics and rogues and Fools and we must and shall and will defend ourselves.[42]

Since Jackson saw the survival of the Union as the basic issue in the nullification crisis, it was no wonder that he suspected those who had so recently attacked the Union, and stood by those who had aided him in its defense. Perhaps, on the day he wrote the letter to Coffee, he remembered the words of Randolph and those of Senator George M. Dallas of Pennsylvania, who had written in the midst of the crisis, "Those who but yesterday opposed your re-election with ferocity now loudly profess their reliance on your saving the Union." [43]

It is not to be implied that Jackson, as President, chose to dis-associate himself from the slave interests. In 1831 he had instructed Martin Van Buren, in a letter marked "Private and confidential", to "feel the British minister" on the possibility of a treaty to allow citizens to reclaim fugitive slaves from Canada.[44] As has been shown, during his years as chief executive he had remained in close contact with events on his plantations and continued to buy and sell slaves. What is evident is that Jackson refused to allow the issue of slavery to interfere with his desire to protect and expand the Union. In 1820 he had attacked Northerners, in 1823 Southerners, and in 1835 he again lashed out at elements who, in their passion over the issue of slavery, threatened to disturb the peace and safety of "our happy country". In a letter to Postmaster General Kendall, Jackson attacked the use of the mails by abolitionists to flood the South with literature which would "stir up amongst the South the horrors of a servile war". These men he termed "monsters", but he also admonished those who, in their desire to destroy the inflammatory tracts, had broken into the post office at Charleston and seized the mail:

This spirit of mob-law is becoming too common and must be checked, or ere long it will become as great an evil as a servile war . . . the instigators

---

42 *Ibid.,* IV, 421-22 (March 18, 1832).
43 *Ibid.,* 496 (December 6, 1832).
44 *Ibid.,* 385 (December 17, 1831).

of both [mob law and servile war] must be checked and punished, or we will soon have no safety under our happy Government of laws.[45]

Jackson ordered that the papers be delivered only to those who demanded them as subscribers, and that the names of these people be published in the newspaper. "This would bring those in the South, who were patronizing these incendiary works to such disrepute with all the South, that they would be compelled to desist, or move from the country." [46]

Thus, Northerners and Southerners, abolitionists and their most violent opponents felt the cane of Old Hickory, the Union's man. It is interesting that Jackson recognized the abolition movement to be of some political significance and saw some dangers in its methods. However, he never appears to have considered the movement in terms of its ultimate stated goal. The years between his retirement from office and his death coincided with the steady growth of the movement, and yet there is no evidence that he became alarmed at the possibility that it would some day succeed in overthrowing the economic and social system of which he was a part. To the former President the anti-slavery movement had some relevancy to election campaigns and the Texas annexation movement, but apparently none at all to the status of his Negroes at the Hermitage.

In the Presidential campaign of 1840 Jackson recognized abolition as an issue which could be utilized against the Whigs. Writing in support of Van Buren, he stated, "From General H — s conduct I have always viewed him as a Federalist, and now believe him an abolitionist." [47] He obviously felt that the issue would be a boon to Van Buren's prospects in Tennessee. He told Andrew J. Donelson that things were going well for the Democrats in his home district. "I have no fears of the result. The abolition questions begins to draw the attention, I may say the serious attention of the people here." [48]

The last great campaign in which the old general found himself involved was the conflict over Texas annexation. Not willing to endanger the Union, Jackson had avoided pressing the battle during the last years of his administration. Because at that time the slavery issue was in the forefront of the annexation debates, Jackson, the nationalist, was unwilling to make a stand. When David G. Burnet,

[45] *Ibid.*, V, 360 (August 9, 1835).
[46] *Ibid.*, 360-61.
[47] *Ibid.*, VI, 68, To F. M. Dancy and Thomas B. M. Murphy (July 3, 1840).
[48] *Ibid.*, 79 (October 8, 1840).

ANDREW JACKSON AND THE NEGRO 133

President *ad interim* of the Republic of Texas, in 1836 sent him a letter justifying annexation on sectional and political grounds, Jackson repudiated the argument, stating that nationalism was the only sufficient basis for such a policy.[49] The North and East would have to be presented with an incentive that would offset their antagonism to the spread of slavery. The President could offer only one way whereby Texas annexation could bind the Union together rather than rend it apart: "Texas must claim the Californias. The fishing interests of the North and East wish a harbor on the Pacific." [50]

In the 1840's, with Great Britain's role in Texan affairs growing, Jackson recognized both the need and the opportunity to strike. Now annexation could be stressed as a matter of national welfare. Northern commercial interests would be as unhappy as Southern slaveholders at the prospect of a British-dominated Texas. In 1843 Jackson wrote, "It must be a traitor to our country and its best interests who will vote against . . . a bill authorizing the President to enter into a negotiation with Texas for its annexation to the United States." [51] Jackson attacked those who continued publicly to tie Texas to the slavery issue:

Mr. Calhoun . . . has displayed a great weakness and folly to introduce . . . matter that did not belong to the subject and well calculated to arouse the Eastern states against the annexation of Texas. The power of the states over slavery was not necessary by him then to have been brought into view. How many men of talent want good common sense.[52]

Despite his denial that slavery was the primary issue at hand and his realization that, if made such, it could mean defeat in achieving annexation, Jackson once more did not hesitate to employ it in such

[49] Bassett, *The Life of Jackson*, 678, citing a letter in Van Buren MSS., without date, endorsed by Van Buren, "President's Letter". Burnet held the office during the spring and summer of 1836.
[50] Marquis James, *Andrew Jackson: Portrait of a President* (Indianapolis, Bobbs-Merrill Co., 1937), 424, citing George P. Garrison (ed.), *Diplomatic Correspondence of the Republic of Texas* (1908), I, 194-95, W. H. Wharton to T. J. Rush, Secretary of State, Texas Republic, undated, but about February 15, 1837. Wharton, Envoy Extraordinary and Minister Plenipotentiary of the Republic of Texas, heard these words during an interview with the President.
[51] Bassett, *Correspondence*, VI, 230, To Major William B. Lewis (September 18, 1843).
[52] *Ibid.*, 287, To Francis P. Blair (May 11, 1844). Some annexationists suspected Calhoun of more than a lack of common sense. Francis Blair, editor of the Washington *Globe*, and Thomas Hart Benton believed he and his associates were using the Texas issue to split the Union and create a new confederacy of slaveholding states; *ibid.*, 301, From Francis P. Blair (July 7, 1844).

a way as might prove beneficial to his cause. To the public, British intrigue in Texas was to be described as dangerous to the interests of the United States in general, but certain Southerners were to be reminded privately that their interests in particular were threatened. Jackson urged his friend Major William B. Lewis to exert pressure on Tyler via the President's confidant, Senator Robert J. Walker of Mississippi, and to stress the consequences of Texas becoming a British protectorate. He suggested the following line of argument: "Would not . . . our slaves in the great valley of the Mississippi, [be] worth nothing, because they would all run over to Texas and under British influence, [be] liberated and lost to their owners?" [53] Jackson also urged Francis P. Blair, editor of the Washington *Globe*, to arouse influential Southerners and Westerners to the dangers of British abolitionist influence in Texas.[54]

Perhaps Jackson, as a slaveholder, was concerned to some extent with the possible effects of a change in the status of the institution in Texas upon his own economic interest and those of his neighbors. However, a letter which he wrote to his nephew Andrew J. Donelson, who was at the time chargé d'affaires to the Texas Republic, indicates that he saw British influence a threat to the nation as a whole as well as to slaveholders. He predicted that, if Texas was not joined to the United States, within six years it would become a province of Great Britain. British immigration would follow and with it the abolition of slavery. Under such conditions war with the United States was certain.[55]

There is no evidence that Jackson's desire for expansion into Texas was influenced by any personal interest in the expansion of slavery. He used the slavery issue cautiously and in the negative sense of protecting the institution where it already existed. On the question of expansion, Jackson appears to have been first and foremost a nationalist. The growth of the Union is what he desired. He considered the man who stood in the way of acquiring Oregon as much a traitor as the man who opposed Texas annexation.[56] Slavery was a divisive issue, and anyone who insisted upon agitating over it had no place in the administration of the federal government. When

[53] *Ibid.*, 278 (April 8, 1844).
[54] *Ibid.*, 283 (May 7, 1844).
[55] *Ibid.*, 335, December 2, 1844.
[56] *Ibid.*, 230, To Major William B. Lewis (September 18, 1843).

Tyler suggested to President-elect Polk that a cabinet post be given to Calhoun, Jackson wrote, "You could not get on with him. England is the place for him, there to combat with my Lord Aberdeen, the abolition question." [57]

In his attitude toward the Negro problem, Andrew Jackson reflected both the glory of his era and the tragedy that was to come. Accepting slavery's existence as necessary to his economic way of life, he viewed any attempt to enter the Negro into the mainstream of politics as an act of selfish political intent with consequences destructive to the Union he revered. His position helped keep a national party together and expand the territory of the United States. However, while he failed to recognize the moral intensity of the issue, less responsible individuals were fanning the flames of dissension and creating a fire which the weaker and less dedicated chieftains who followed were unable to extinguish.

If it is regrettable that Andrew Jackson was unable to recognize the early stirrings of slavery agitation as involving more than selfish politics, it is at least understandable in the light of his own experiences. His attitude toward the Negro appears to have been governed at all times by immediate and practical expediency. Whether in the fields of commerce, plantation management, military tactics or politics, he used the Negro to facilitate the attainment of his immediate objectives. Economic success, military victory and the preservation and growth of the Union were goals which this practical man could understand and desire. It would not be unreasonable to suspect that Jackson viewed the agitation of the abolitionist and slavery expansion forces as similar to the tactics he employed in his messages to the free Negroes of Louisiana in 1814, emotional appeals to attain short-range practical goals. He appears to have been more a tactician than a strategist, cognizant of the immediate plans of these forces and the immediate dangers incumbent in them, without recognizing their long term objectives, purposes, and social value. He thought of the Negro in the present tense and appreciated him primarily as a tool in hand. He seems to have been unable to comprehend that some looked upon the Negro slave as the necessary foundation of a great civilization, and still others looked upon him as a human being denied the basic human rights.

[57] December 16, 1844, *Polk Papers*, Library of Congress, cited by Bassett, *The Life of Jackson*, 746-47.

CHAPTER VI

ANDREW JACKSON AND THE INDIAN

If one desires to see Andrew Jackson as a rugged Westerner with a sword in one hand and a pistol in the other, he need only examine the General's contact with the Indian. It was a relationship based upon a relatively simple syllogism: Jackson was an expansionist; the Indian was a present and visible obstacle to this expansion; Jackson favored the removal of this obstacle in the most expeditious manner possible.

As early as January 30, 1793, Jackson offered a view regarding negotiations with Indians, which was to be maintained throughout his life. In a letter to John McKee, who had been sent by Tennessee's Governor Blount to talk peace with the Cherokees, Jackson questioned the policy of negotiating with a tribe which he claimed failed to adhere to past agreements. ". . . why do we attempts to treat with Savage Tribes that will neither adhere to Treaties, nor the law of Nations . . . ?" [1]

One need not be an authority on Indian affairs to be taken aback by Jackson's argument. Over and over again, before and after the date of this letter, treaties were made with the red men, violated by the whites and new treaties written to legalize the violations. Whites, and not Indians, were the first to break the Treaty of 1791, to which Jackson alluded in his letter. In 1793 a military foray from Nashville, impatient with the delays of diplomatic negotiations, in defiance of Federal law, crushed the Cherokees in Tennessee and opened their land to settlement.[2] Jackson himself took advantage of the violation of the treaty. In 1795 he journeyed to Philadelphia to sell and profit from his share of the spoils. His partner, John Overton, wrote:

[1] Bassett, *Correspondence*, I, 12.
[2] George Dewey Harmon, *Sixty Years of Indian Affairs* (Chapel Hill, The University of North Carolina Press, 1941), 46.

When you sell land it [is] my wish that you be candid and unreserved with the purchasers, with respect to the situation and quality of the Land and particularly inform them that they are situated without the [boundaries of land opened to white settlement by the] Treaty of Holston [Treaty of 1791]. . . .[3]

Despite Jackson's obvious exaggeration regarding treaty breaking in the letter to McKee, it is likely that his motives for making the statement were based upon firmly held convictions that the Indian nations were not entitled to be treated as foreign independent powers, and that the land upon which they lived deservedly belonged to those who could utilize it to its maximum efficiency, namely the white man. These convictions are illustrated, though not always stated, in numerous contacts which Jackson had with the race. Unlike Jefferson, he does not appear to have had an inner conflict to resolve, involving a desire to do right by both white and red men at the same time. What conflict he did have was between what he saw as the practical law of the frontier, which quickly opened land for settlement (and speculation), and the impractical law of the nation, which, by recognizing Indian sovereignty, impeded white man's destiny.

Whatever conclusions might be drawn regarding Andrew Jackson's attitude toward the Indian, it cannot be argued that he arrived at it second hand. Every schoolboy knows that he was an Indian fighter. It is a rather interesting phenomenon that, while most textbooks will admit that our treatment of the Indian was a black mark in history, they still pay homage to those who made the greatest contributions to the virtual eradication of that race, the Davy Crocketts, General Custers and Andrew Jacksons.

When Andrew Jackson went to war against the Indian, he did so in the spirit of the Westerner, employing the white man's war whoop of invectives. Upon learning of the unleashing of what he called Tecumseh's "deceitful and ruthless savages", his "unrelenting barbarians", Jackson declared to William Henry Harrison, *"The Blood of our murdered heroes must be revenged* that Banditti ought to be swept from the face of the earth." [4]

Jackson had his greatest opportunity to apply this tactical advice during the long drawn-out Creek Wars. An early incident of the conflict involved the capture by the Indians of a white woman. Jack-

[3] Bassett, *Correspondence*, I, 13 (March 8, 1795).
[4] *Ibid.*, 210 (November 30, 1811).

son outlined his plan for a rescue operation to the Governor of Tennessee, Willie Blount. He would invade the Creek towns and follow the "justifiable" tactic of "laying waste their villages, burning their houses, killing their warriors and leading into captivity their wives and children" until he obtained "a surrender of the captive and the captors". Not treaties but "a combined movement and sudden blow" was Jackson's formula for "eternal peace with the southern tribes".[5]

It is interesting to note that when engaged in Indian warfare, the language and tactical outlook of Jackson, the so-called Indian hater, and the humanitarian Jefferson were quite similar. Like Jefferson, Jackson at times recognized the value of gaining Indian allies, and in the Creek War and War of 1812 successfully employed Cherokees, Choctaws, Chickasaws and friendly Creeks against the enemy. Even his attitude toward the method of dealing with potential Indian allies was basically the same as Jefferson's. Writing to Willie Blount on June 17, 1812, Jackson stated:

I heartily concur with you in your ideas with respect to the little confidence that ought to be placed in the aid or friendschip of Indians. . . .

If we get the Cherokees engaged with the Creeks, they will be obliged to be friendly with us to preserve themselves. I believe self interest and self preservation the most predominant passion, fear is better than love with an Indian.[6]

There was not the slightest hint of romanticism in General Jackson's reports of the actions of his Indian allies. With a military man's appreciation and respect for gallantry in battle, he was quick to praise their bravery when he observed it.[7] However, he was also well aware of the shortcomings of his aboriginal allies. "The inconvenience attending Indians is, that you cannot keep them in the field, as soon as they perform an excursion, and take a scalp, they must go home and have a dance."[8]

The apparent absence of any deep-seated humanitarian concern by Jackson for the Indians as a race enabled him to be governed at

[5]   *Ibid.*, 230 (July 3, 1812).
[6]   *Ibid.*, 228.
[7]   *Ibid.*, 341, To Willie Blount (November 4, 1813), and *ibid.*, 489, To Thomas Pinckney (March 28, 1814). In both letters Jackson spoke of actions of the Cherokees in battle, using the term "great bravery" in the former and "gallantry" in the latter.
[8]   *Ibid.*, II, 101-2, To Secretary Monroe (November 20, 1814).

all times by practical expediency in his dealings with them. Thus, actions which might seem contradictory if they were performed by a Jefferson, appear quite consistent in the light of Old Hickory's pragmatism. Such an approach enabled him, with probably clear conscience, to cast covetous eyes upon the lands of the Cherokees and Chickasaws at the same time he was employing them as allies in battle. The war which caused Jackson to call upon these nations for military assistance also provided an excuse to grab off their tribal claims in Tennessee:

now is the time, and I hope will seize holt of it, to extinguish the cherokee and chikesaw claim within the state of T. It can be with truth said to the chikesaws you have proved to us, that you cannot protect the whites on the road through your country. The enemy you have permitted to pass through your nation have killed and plunder our citizens, carried off our women and children captives. we must therefore extend our settlement to the mississippi, to cut off all communication of the southern tribes with that of the north, and give to our citizens perfect safety in passing through their country.[9]

In the summer of 1814 the hero of Horseshoe Bend was given power to establish the terms of peace with the Creek nation. To Fort Jackson came the Creeks who had fought beside him and expected their due reward as well as the few remaining Red Sticks, who had chosen the wrong side. Addressing both Red Sticks and allies as "Friends and Brothers", he told them that the war had been expensive, and to pay for it and avert the possibility of future war, the United States would have to indemnify itself with land from the whole Creek nation.[10] To the shocked Indians he put forth terms which one biographer has termed "unequal for exorbitance".[11] Approximately twenty million acres of Georgia and Alabama land was the price demanded from friend and foe alike. On August 9, 1814, the treaty was signed by thirty-six chiefs, one of whom had been a Red Stick.[12] The next day Jackson informed his wife that the "disagreeable business" had been accomplished.[13]

[9]   *Ibid.*, 3, To Major-General Thomas Pinckney (May 18, 1814).
[10] Marquis James, *Andrew Jackson, The Border Captain*, 188, citing Jackson Papers, Library of Congress.
[11] *Ibid.*, 189.
[12] For text of the treaty see *American State Papers, Indian Affairs* (Washington, Gales and Seaton, 1832-1834), I, 826. For discussion of treaty see Harmon, *Sixty Years*, 143-50.
[13] James, *Border Captain*, 190, citing private collection of Oliver R. Bassett, Chicago.

Disagreeable but, in his mind, necessary actions like those at Fort Jackson or the whipping of an insubordinate slave at the Hermitage never appear to have stayed the course of Old Hickory. William Crawford, appointed Secretary of War in 1816, was to learn that the price of blocking Jackson's way was to earn his eternal disdain. Their first clash occurred after Crawford learned that among the twenty million acres acquired in the Treaty of Fort Jackson were four million rightfully belonging to the Cherokees and Chickasaws. The Secretary ordered the land returned and directed Jackson to remove the squatters who had occupied it.[14] Jackson denied the validity of the Indian claim and reminded Crawford that many of the squatters whom he had been ordered to remove were veterans of the recent wars:

I say whenever these very people are to be removed from the Villages of the hostile Creek, which was the den of the murderers of our wives and children, find their land to be given once more to the prowling lion of the forest who has done us so much injury, your forebodings will be like mine, that the worst of consequences may flow. . . .[15]

Crawford's reply, in so many words, stated that the squatters would be removed and that Jackson would enforce the removal.[16] In the end, growing friction between the Indians and squatters and pressure from the Westerners caused Madison to appoint Jackson, along with David Merryweather and Jesse Franklin, als commissioners to negotiate with the Indians. Though still insisting that the Indians' claim was invalid, Jackson accepted the task. The objective was the land and the General was willing to change his tactics to attain it. He told Secretary of State James Monroe, "I have but little doubt if a proper application was made to the cherokees, they would yield up all pretention to this Territory for a very small compensation." [17]

Jackson's prediction proved correct. His satisfaction at the results of the negotiation and the value he placed upon the acquired land were conveyed in a letter written to Monroe:

. . . all these conflicting claims are happily accomodated by the late treaties with those tribes at the moderate premium of 180,000 dollars . . . in which is included . . . that extensive and fertile country lying north of the Tennessee. This territory added to the creek cession, opens an avenue to the defense of the lower country, in a political point of view incalculable,

[14]   Bassett, *Correspondence*, II, 227 (January 27, 1816).
[15]   *Ibid.*, 248 (June, 1816).
[16]   *Ibid.*, 251 (July 1, 1816).
[17]   *Ibid.*, 252-53 (July 8, 1816).

we will have now good roads, well supplied by the industry of our own citizens, and our frontier defended by a strong population . . . and [the sale of the land] will bring into the treasury immense sums of money. . . .[18]

Firmly established as a national hero, Andrew Jackson could speak to Presidents and expect to be heard. On March 4, 1817, he addressed a lengthy letter to President Monroe in which he put forth his views of what should be the proper relationship between the United States government and the several Indian nations. Recognizing that what he was about to propose would amount to a radical change in government procedure, he began by saying to the President, "I beg you will not be astonished at the grounds I assume until you examine it well." [19]

He then expressed his belief that treaties with the Indians were "an absurdity", since the red men were subjects of the United States, inhabiting its territory and acknowledging its sovereignty. If Congress could legislate for the territories, made up of citizens of the United States, it could certainly legislate for the Indians, who were subjects, entitled only to protection and care. He contended that Congress had the "right to prescribe their bounds at pleasure" and "whenever the safety, interest or defense of the country should render it necessary for the Government of the United States to occupy and possess any part of the Territory, used by them for hunting, that they have the right to take it and dispose of it." [20]

Jackson went on to point out that, if a citizen could be deprived of his land by the government's right of eminent domain, certainly an Indian, "thrown on the bounty of the Government, subject to its sovereignty, not possessing the right of soil or Domain merely having the possessory right yielded by the liberality of the United States through humanity", should be subject to the same law. Jackson insisted that the Indians did not exist as an independent nation and the policy and practice of treating them as such had been based on the "weakness of the arm of Government" rather than any right possessed by the tribes.[21]

He concluded his argument with a brief dissertation upon the need for the Indians to surrender their hunting lands and turn to agri-

[18] *Ibid.*, 261 (October 23, 1816).
[19] *Ibid.*, 279.
[20] *Ibid.*
[21] *Ibid.*, 279-80.

culture as the road to civilization.[22] This part of the letter offered
nothing new. Such talk had become standard operating procedure
for providing a rationale by those who coveted Indian land, as well
as those sincerely interested in the Indians' welfare. There is little
doubt that Jackson belonged among the former, for his stated purpose
for the entire discussion had been to point out to the President
"how ... land is to be obtained from the Indians, they having refused
to relinquish their claim ...".[23]

Two letters written by Jackson in 1826 provide a rather good idea
of what his concern for the "safety interest, or defense of the country"
meant for the civilized Indian nations of the South. In the first he
stated, "This section of country is of great importance to the prosperity
and strength of the lower Mississippi, a dense white population would
add much to its safety in a state of war." [24] In the second he proclaimed, "What is the value of the soil compared to the value of the
population that section of the country will maintain. Labour is the
wealth of all nations. ..." [25]

The views Andrew Jackson put forth in his letter to President
Monroe might be considered a ruthless attempt to remove the last
vestige of self-determination from the hands of the Indians. Jefferson
had been shocked at the idea of subjecting the Indians to our laws
without their consent, "when a little patience and money" were "so
rapidly accomplishing their voluntary removal beyond the Mississippi".[26] Considering the fate which Jefferson and other responsible
leaders envisioned for the Indians — ultimate removal to the West —
the only real sin which Jackson could be singled out for is that of
impatience, the impatience of a determined and wholly practical
man. Being such, he could realize that legality can, at times, be
synonomous with inefficiency and even provide a facade for corruption. Jackson, termed Indian hater, pointed out one result of a policy
encouraged by the Sage of Monticello:

... money, is the weapon, in the hands of the commissioner, wielded to

[22] *Ibid.*, 280-81.
[23] *Ibid.*, 279. Jackson was referring specifically to the Chickasaw land on the
east bank of the Mississippi in the state of Kentucky. Surrender of this land by
the Indians "would not only cut off all intercourse between northern Indians,
and the Chickasaws and Choctaws, but insure safety to our commerce on the
Ohio and Mississippi, and afford a strong defence within striking distance of the
settlements on the Mississippi and Missouri Rivers" (*Ibid.*, 278-79).
[24] *Ibid.*, III, 312, To Brigadier-General John Coffee (September 2, 1826).
[25] *Ibid.*, 315, To Brigadier-General John Coffee (September 25, 1826).
[26] Ford, *Works*, X, 115, To Albert Gallatin (November 24, 1818).

corrupt a few of their leaders, and induce them to adopt the plans embraced by the views of the Government, when the poor of the nation receive but little, and are, by the influence of their Chiefs, (thus managed by corruption) induced to assent to their wills.[27]

When one reads the responses to Jackson's suggestions by men of some standing, it becomes rather obvious that Old Hickory was not necessarily considered a wild-eyed frontiersman by his contemporaries. President Monroe wrote:

The views which you have taken of the Indian title to lands is very new but very deserving of attention. ... A compulsory process seems to be necessary, to break their habits and to civilize them, and there is much cause to believe that it must be resorted to, to preserve them.[28]

In 1820 and 1821 Jackson had repeated his views on treaties to John C. Calhoun, and received the following reply:

... I entirely concur with you that it is perfectly absurd to hold treaties with those within our limits as they neither are or can be independent of our government. This opinion has been frequently communicated to Congress, and altho' they have not yet adopted it, I still hope they will ultimately.[29]

Between the years 1817 and 1829 Jackson was involved in treaty-making with each of the major Indian nations of the South: Cherokee, Creek, Chickasaw, Choctaw and Seminole. The formula for each negotiation was essentially the same. The Indians were told that they were not sovereign, that they could no longer live as independent nations within the boundaries of white settlements, that they had the choice of remaining as farmers on six hundred and forty acres for each family, subject to the laws of the state, or moving beyond the Mississippi, where they could maintain their identity as a nation. Jackson recognized that the threat to Indian nationhood was an effective incentive for their emigration and used it consistently in the negotiations.[30] Writing to Calhoun in 1820, in reference to the

[27] Bassett, *Correspondence*, II, 281, To the President (James Monroe) (March 4, 1817).
[28] *Ibid.*, 331-32 (October 5, 1817).
[29] *Ibid.*, III, 132, From Secretary Calhoun (November 16, 1821), Jackson had expressed his views on treaties to Calhoun in letters dated September 20, 1820 (*Ibid.*, 31), and January 18, 1821 (*Ibid.*, 371).
[30] For Jackson's activities as a commissioner to treat with the Indians, see Bassett, *Correspondence*, II, 299, 300, 307, 388, 399, 405, 414; III, 23, 27, 31, 118-21, 132, 371.

forthcoming deliberatons with the Choctaws, he stated, "The pride of a real Indian is in the strength of his Nation and this is the chord I mean to touch to obtain the object in view." He planned to describe the new lands as a place "where their father the President of the U. States means to settle his red children — concentrate and perpetuate them as a nation and thereby make his children happy." [31]

To Colonel John D. Terrill, who in 1826 had been appointed special agent to prepare the Chickasaws for a cession of their land, Jackson sent some advice, urging "attention to Indian character":

> ... with them, as with all Indians, the best plan will be to come out with candor, tell them, situated where they now are, that they will always be exposed to encroachment from the white people. ... Say to them, their Father, the President will lay off a country of equal extent, transport them to it, and give besides a premium of money which will enable them to buy stock etc.; that he will establish land marks for them never to be moved, and give them a free simple title to the land. You must be prepared to give assurance of permanency of title, and dwell upon the idea that they will never be asked to surrender an acre more. It might not then be useless to bring to their view the hope of a union between the Choctaws, Creeks and Chickasaws, as a speedy means of making them a great, powerful, and happy people and, when their children shall be educated, of enabling them to become a member of the United States, as Alabama and Mississippi are. With these hints I shall only add that you should be careful to promise nothing, but what you will religiously perform, or they will say to you, you lye too.[32]

Jackson was convinced that the Indians must be shown the hopelessness of their situation within the states, if the government was ever to offset the influence of tribesmen who urged them to hold fast to their lands.[33] Though Jackson's statements to the Indians regarding their loss of sovereignty and independence had never been supported by Congressional action, nevertheless, when he told the chiefs that, if they stayed, their white neighbors would constantly encroach upon their domain, he spoke the truth. There was nothing fair about being pressured to remove from one's lands. However, those who took Jackson's advice probably avoided the agony that was later to befall the Cherokees at the hands of their Georgia neighbors.

Considering Jackson's pronouncements and deeds regarding the Indians throughout the years, it is not surprising that as President

---

[31]   *Ibid.*, III, 27-28 (June 19, 1820).
[32]   *Ibid.*, II, 308-9 (July 28, 1826).
[33]   *Ibid.*, 388, To Isaac Shelby (August 11, 1818).

he sought to continue and hasten the policy of removal which had
been accepted by President Monroe.[34] Nor is it surprising that when
states decided to extend their sovereignty over the Indians within
their borders, Jackson supported the moves even in the face of a
Supreme Court decision.

In a letter to Captain James Gadsden, his friend and former aide
of the Florida campaign, Jackson, on October 12, 1829, briefly described the Indian policy he intended to pursue as President:

I have recommended them to quit their possession on this side of the
Mississippi and go to a country in the west where there is every probability
that they will always be free from the mercenary influence of the White
men, and undisturbed by the local authority of the states: Under such
circumstances the General Government can exercise a parental control over
their interests and possibly perpetuate them in their race.[35]

In his First Annual Message to Congress, Jackson spoke of the "incompatible" policy toward the Indians pursued by the government
in the past, by which the civilized arts had been encouraged on one
hand while on the other they had been pressured to remove from
their lands to the wilderness, and thus revert back to savagery. Turning to the Indians of Alabama and Georgia, he acknowledged the
progress they had made toward civilization, but in the same breath
encouraged the establishment of lands in the West for their resettlement. Reversing the stand of John Quincy Adams, he stood by the
governments of interested states in their determination to exert
sovereignty over the tribes within their borders.[36]

Recognizing that he was recommending a policy which sounded
quite similar to the one he had just condemned, Jackson promised
different results. The Indians would be guaranteed their new lands
"as long as they shall occupy it, each tribe having a distinct control
over the portion designated for its use". He implied to Congress that
the long history of broken promises would finally come to an end:

There [in the West] they may be secured in the enjoyment of governments
of their own choice, subject to no other control from the US than such
as may be necessary to preserve peace on the frontier and between the
several tribes. There the benevolent may endeavor to teach them the arts
of civilization, and, by promoting union and harmony among them, to

[34]   Note page 118 for Monroe's statement regarding the impossibility of incorporating the Indians into "our system".
[35]   Bassett, *Correspondence*, IV, 8.
[36]   Richardson, *Messages*, II, 456-58 (December 8, 1829).

raise up an interesting commonwealth, destined to perpetuate the race and to attest to the humanity and justice of this Govt.[37]

Jackson promised that any emigration should be voluntary, recognizing the hardships involved in moving to a distant land. However, he insisted that the choice for the Indians was either removal or submission to the laws of the states.[38]

What this address implied was that the demands of the frontier would be met in the present. At the same time, the "benevolent" friends of the Indians were reassured that the future belonged to them. Jackson's words painted a rosy picture even for those red men who desired to stay, under certain conditions. "Submitting to the laws of the State and receiving, like other citizens, protection in their persons and property, they will ere long become merged in the mass of our population." [39]

In truth, the message signaled that the Western attitude toward the Indian problem was firmly established in the White House. The language of the treaty council was being expounded in the messages of the Chief Executive. For all the talk of the future happiness of the Indians, the only immediate beneficiaries of Jackson's policy could be the whites. It is difficult to imagine that one who had been instrumental in removing Indians from their guaranteed lands could truly believe that the Indians would in the West find permanent rest from the white man's greed. It is difficult to imagine that one who recognized that the "pride of a real Indian is in the strength of his nation" and who had acknowledged the tendency of whites to exploit the Indian could visualize the possibility of the Indians being "ere long merged in the mass of our population". What appears probable is that Jackson, the tactician, was primarily concerned with overcoming the immediate obstacles to his goal of a white populated country east of the Mississippi. One barrier was the Indian possession of large tracts of fertile land and demand for nationhood within the states; the other appears to have been, to use Jackson's term, "the benevolent", whose numbers were being increased with each passing day of the struggle between the Indians and the states of Alabama, Georgia and Mississippi.[40]

[37] *Ibid.*
[38] *Ibid.*, 458-59.
[39] *Ibid.*
[40] George Harmon wrote, "While William Lloyd Garrison was using his pen to arouse the people against the evils of Negro slavery at this time, the people were indifferent to his cause. But the case of the poor Cherokee had aroused the whole country." (*Sixty Years,* 187).

There are two rather interesting letters among Jackson's papers which tend to indicate that by 1830 Western public opinion was firmly committed to removal. The first is from Jackson's Tennessee neighbor, Alfred Balch. He wrote:

The removal of the Indians would be an act of seeming violence. But it will prove in the end an act of enlarged philanthropy. These untutored sons of the Forest, cannot exist in a state of Independence, in the vicinity of the white man. If they will persist in remaining where they are they may begin to dig their own graves and prepare to die.[41]

The couching of acts of injustice toward the Indians in terms of humanity and philanthropy is exceeded in its ludicrousness only by the terming of efforts by the Indians to save what was rightfully theirs as self-imposed destruction. The *humane* tone of this letter is repeated in the second, written by Jackson to an interpreter among the Choctaws in Mississippi:

I beg you to say to them, that their *interest happiness* peace and prosperity depend upon their removal beyond the jurisdiction of the laws of the State of Mississippi. ... I feel conscious of having done my duty to my red children and if any failure of my good intention arises, it will be attributed to their want of duty to themselves, not to me.[42]

It is interesting to note that, less than a year after his First Annual Message, Jackson was acknowledging the impossibility of the Indians living under the jurisdiction of the state. He had already stood firmly opposed to their independence within the state. Thus, it appears that, despite earlier assurances that the Indians were to be given a choice, Jackson was by 1830 committed to a policy of complete removal.

A very good reason for Jackson's failure to again mention the possibility of the Indians becoming "merged in the mass of our population" was the events which ensued in Georgia and Alabama just after he sent his First Annual Message to Congress. The legislature of Georgia extended its authority over the Cherokees, nullifying all previous treaties and annexing their territories, and Alabama showed signs of moving in the same direction relative to the Creeks.[43] When the Indians hired former Attorney General William Wirt to demand

[41] Bassett, *Correspondence,* IV, 116 (January 8, 1830).
[42] *Ibid.,* 169, To John Pitchlyn (August 5, 1830).
[43] Harmon, *Sixty Years,* 184, citing Moses Dawson, *Compilation of the Laws of the State of Georgia (1829),* 29-198. Georgia's ruling went into effect on January 1, 1830.

that the United States protect their treaty rights, Jackson exploded:

The Creeks have officially informed us that they will not meet us. We have
answered, that we leave them to themselves, and to the protection of their
friend Mr. Wirt, to whose protection they look, and to whom they have
given a large fee to protect them in their rights as an independent Nation;
and when they find that they cannot live under the laws of Alabama, they
must find, at their own expense, and by their means, a country and a
home. The course of Mr. Wirt has been truly wicked. It has been wielded
as an engine to prevent the Indians from moving X the Mississippi and
will lead to the destruction of the poor ignorant Indians. It must be so, I
have used all the persuasive means in my power. I have exonerated the
national character from all imputation, and now leave the poor deluded
Creeks and Cherokees to their fate, and their annihilation, which their
wicked advisers has induced.[44]

Jackson claimed that the advisors to the Indians, "all the missionary
and speculating tribe", were waiting for "the Executive" to make
greater offers so that they might make huge financial profits at the
expense of the United States.[45]

Recognizing that a judicial decision might possibly place him in
the embarrassing position of having to choose between supporting
the ruling of the Supreme Court or nullification by the states, Jackson
was eager to press for removal. His Second Annual Message reflected
the situation. There were some interesting changes in his expressed
attitudes toward the history of the Government's Indian policy and
the future of that race. He spoke of removal as the "consummation
of a policy originating at an early period, and steadily pursued by
every administration within the present century – so justified to the
States and so generous to the Indians". Absent were references to
past attempts at civilizing the Indians and, understandably, he did
not draw the attention of Congress to the great progress along those
lines achieved by the Cherokees and Creeks. Only in the West,
separated by distance from the white man, was there a possibility
for eventual civilization.[46]

The federal government, he insisted, had no more right to interfere
with the state's control of the Indians within their boundaries than
they had in meddling in the internal affairs of some foreign nation.
He offered no ifs, ands, or buts about removal. The word "voluntary"

[44] Bassett, *Correspondence*, IV, 176-77, To Major William B. Lewis (August 24,
1830).
[45] *Ibid.*
[46] Richardson, *Messages*, II, 519 ff. (December 6, 1830).

did not appear. The Indian, he declared, "was unwilling to submit to the laws of the States and mingle with their population". The "kindly" government, therefore, offered the red man an opportunity to save himself from "perhaps utter annihilation" by giving him a new home and footing the whole bill for his removal and resettlement.[47]

It seems that all the elements of the Westerner in Jackson are expressed in clearer form in this speech than in any other public address as President. After reading these words, the stranger to American history probably would not be too surprised to learn that the President had been a land speculator, Indian fighter, and was a nationalist with a marked bent toward expansionism. In glowing terms he declared that the treaties for removal recently signed with the Chickasaws and Choctaws, in addition to the "pecuniary advantages" they would bring to the United States and the end they would put to all possible danger of collision between state and federal governments, would:

... place a dense and civilized population in large tracts of country now occupied by a few savage hunters ... strengthen the southwestern frontier and render the adjacent states strong enough to repel future invasion without remote aid ... relieve the whole state of Mississippi and the western part of Alabama of Indian occupancy, and enable the states to advance rapidly in population, wealth and power.[48]

There was a note of eager anticipation in his words, accompanied by impatience with those who saw the plight of the Indians as cause for sympathy. Jackson acknowledged the personal difficulties involved in removal from one's home, but pointed out that they were no more difficult than those faced by the white colonists who crossed the seas to find new opportunities far removed from their places of birth:

And is it supposed that the wandering savage has a stronger attachment to his home than the settled, civilized Christian? Is it more afflicting to leave the graves of his fathers than it is to our brothers and children ... ? If the offers made to the Indian were extended to [our own people] ... they would be hailed with gratitude and joy.[49]

Jackson was laying the cards on the table. To those with compassion, he warned that the Indians stood on the brink of disaster. He gave

[47] *Ibid.*
[48] *Ibid.*, 519-20.
[49] *Ibid.*, 520-21.

the impression that his plan offered the only chance for them to be saved from "utter annihilation". Only in the West might their existence "be prolonged and perhaps made perpetual". The general would allow the fort to surrender and its troops to march out with their colors flying. But this was war, and in Jackson the West had a spokesman to present its arguments:

> Humanity has often wept over the fate of the aborigines of this country, and Philanthropy has been long busily employed in devising means to avert it, but its progress has never for a moment been arrested, and one by one have many powerful tribes disappeared from the earth. To follow to the tomb the last of his race and to tread on the graves of extinct nations excite melancholy reflections. But true philanthropy reconciles the mind to these vicissitudes as it does to the extinction of one generation to make room for another. . . . Philanthropy could not wish to see this continent restored to the condition in which it was found by our forefathers. What good man would prefer a country covered with forests and ranged by a few thousand savages to our extensive Republic, studded with cities, towns, and prosperous farms, embellished with all the improvements which art can devise or industry execute, occupied by more than 12,000,000 happy people and filled with all the blessings of liberty, civilization and religion.[50]

John Adams had used a similar argument to justify the past; Jackson was here providing justification for what he wished accomplished in the immediate future. On February 22, 1831, he reiterated to Congress the necessity for removal. He insisted that any friend of the Indians would urge them to leave. It was impossible to consider their remaining within the limits of white settlement, for trouble between the races would ensue immediately and constantly.[51]

When the Supreme Court, in the case of *Worcester* vs. *Georgia,* upheld Indian independence, Jackson took it as a personal affront, claiming that "Clay, Calhoun, and Webster ... and the supreme court, have united, to embarrass me".[52] Not choosing the aid those who embarrassed him or to enforce the ruling he found obnoxious, he stood by while the state defied the high tribunal. The man who had used force to achieve so many ends, who had not even hesitated to cross into Spanish Florida to reach a foe, now declared that coercion against Georgia or protection of the Indians within that state

[50] *Ibid.,* 519-20.
[51] *Ibid.,* 536.
[52] Bassett, *Correspondence,* IV, 415, To Colonel Anthony Butler (March 6, 1832).

was impossible. ". . . if orders were issued tomorrow one regiment of militia could not be got to march to save them [Cherokees] from destruction." [53]

As the months passed into years and the Cherokees and part of the Creek nation held firm in their refusal to move, Jackson continued to insist to Congress that peaceful coexistence of the two races within the boundaries of the states was impossible. In his Fifth Annual Message on December 3, 1833, he added fuel to the fire by commenting upon the nature of the Indians. "They have neither the intelligence, the industry, the moral habits, nor the desire of improvement which are essential to any favorable change in their condition." [54]

In such a manner Jackson now spoke of the Cherokees, a nation whose phenomenal progress toward civilization had been attested to by Jefferson twenty-five years earlier. Even Jackson had earlier acknowledged that, as a result of their close contact with the whites, these Indians had "made some progress in the arts of civilized whites".[55] But those sentiments were expressed in 1829, when he had spoken of the possibility of some Indians remaining, recognizing the sovereignty of the state and mingling with the white population. The inexorable positions of both the states and the Indians had since caused him to demand complete removal. The commentary on the general nature of the Indians in the Fifth Annual Message was undoubtedly a reflection of this policy. The question arises as to what extent it was a true reflection of Jackson's personal attitude toward the Indian.

With the exception of commenting upon the Indians' strong sense of nationality and their capacities in war, Jackson apparently had little to say previously about their innate abilities, morals or inner drives. He does not appear to have been given to reflecting upon such topics, and the words of his address, therefore, probably represented the expression of Western prejudice rather than conclusions stemming from anything approaching objective analysis. W. H. Sparks, who obviously took pride in and capitalized on his being reared near Jackson's home, presented a description of the Indian which might serve to illustrate an articulate Western viewpoint:

---

[53] *Ibid.*, 430, To Brigadier-General John Coffee (March 6, 1832).
[54] Richardson, *Messages*, III, 33.
[55] *Ibid.*, II, 457, First Annual Message (December 8, 1829).

They are by nature incapable of that civilization which would enable them to organize governments and teach the science of agriculture. They were formed for the woods, and physically organized to live on flesh. The animals furnishing this were placed with them here, and the only vegetable found with them was the maize, or Indian corn. The white man was organized to feed on vegetables, and they were placed with him in his centre of creation, and he brought them here, and with himself acclimated them, as a necessity, to his existence in America.

No effort can save the red man from extermination that humanity of Christianity may suggest. When deprived of his national food furnished by the forest, he knows not nor can he be taught the means of supplying the want. The capacities of his brain will not admit of the cultivation necessary to that end. And he is done in the presence of civilization, he will know none of its arts; and receiving or commanding none of its results, he will wilt and die.

... The efforts at civilization seem only to reach the mixed bloods, and these only in proportion to the white blood in their veins. The Indian is incapable of the white man's civilization, as indeed all other inferior races are. He has fulfilled his destiny, and is passing away. No approximation of the pursuits or the condition of the white man operates other than as a means of his destruction. It seems his contact is death to every inferior race, when not servile and subject to his care and control.[56]

Andrew Jackson does not appear to have worn such sentiments as these on his sleeve. In fact, there is reason to believe that to a large extent he was drawing upon the prejudiced sentiments of others and utilizing it as a weapon in his hands. Where Jackson displayed a prejudice that was quite his own was in his dedication to white domination of the soil.

There is much in Old Hickory's approach to the Indian to remind one of a military commander's attitude toward the general of a foreign army. If in time of war he is your enemy, defeat him; there is nothing necessarily personal involved. When he has surrendered, treat him as decently as possible; he may some day be your ally. While you are fighting him, you may employ all kinds of invective against him in order to stir your troops to action and perhaps even to put yourself in the proper frame of mind to achieve success in battle. But, after the victory celebrations are over, the emotionalism dies away.

One episode in Jackson's life provides the best evidence to refute charges or suspicions that he was an Indian hater, that he belonged to that fraternity of men who believed that the only good Indian was

[56] Sparks, *Memories of Fifty Years*, 467-68, 478.

a dead one.[57] Only a month before he sent his Fifth Annual Message to Congress, Jackson had written a letter to a Colonel W. Moore in which he told of the circumstances by which he had come to adopt a Creek boy named Lyncoya after the battle of Tallashatchie on November 13, 1813.[58] Going back to the letters of that period we find a communication to Mrs. Jackson in which the General related his motives for adoption and the attitude he expected to be maintained toward the youth:

He is the only branch of his family left, and the others when offered to them to take care of would have nothing to do with him but wanted him to be killed. . . . Charity and Christianity says he ought to be taken care of and I send him to my little Andrew and I hope will adopt him as one of our family.[59]

Jackson's letters indicate that he lavished fatherly attention on Lyncoya, even referring to him as "son".[60] If it were not for the Indian name, no one would suspect that the following words were not written by a white father to his white wife regarding their natural born son: "Tell Lyncoya to read his book and be a good boy and obey you in all things." "Tell Lyncoa I expect him to be a good boy and to hear from you when I come home that he has been so in my absence." [61]

If Jackson had any feelings that the Indians were endowed with an inferior mental capacity, it was not reflected in his attitude toward Lyncoya's education. Writing to Colonel James Gadsden on May 2, 1822, he stated, "I have my little sons including Lyncoya, at school, and their education has been greatly neglected in my absence." [62] In 1823 he wrote to Rachel of his desire to "exhibit" Lyncoya to President Monroe and the Secretary of War, with the intention of having him admitted to West Point when he reached the proper

---

[57] A not untypical description of Jackson is that found in Grace Steele Woodward, *The Cherokees* (Norman, University of Oklahoma Press, 1963), 154, 121. The author writes of Jackson as "the well-known Cherokee hater". She also employs the term "prejudice" in describing his dealings with the Cherokees. "Jackson's prejudice prodigiously multiplied and, in later years, struck cruelly at the heart core of the once powerful Cherokee Nation."

[58] Bassett, *Correspondence*, V, 225 (November 15, 1833).

[59] *Ibid.*, I, 400 (December 19, 1813).

[60] *Ibid.*, II, 358, To Mrs. Jackson (April 8, 1818).

[61] *Ibid.*, III, 220, 241, To Mrs. Jackson (December 28, 1823 and March 27, 1824).

[62] *Ibid.*, 161.

age.[63] The desire for a military education for his Indian son was not to be fulfilled. According to Jackson's biographer, Marquis James, Lyncoya died of tuberculosis in 1827 and was buried in the family plot.[64]

The sufferings of the red men at the hands of Andrew Jackson do not appear to have been the result of the policies of a man prejudiced against their race, but rather of a man whose approach to the Indian problem was basically pragmatic. In his dealings with the tribes and his suggestions to others involved in treaty-making, he had placed primary emphasis on getting land; once this had been obtained, he urged just and liberal payment. Lyncoya was saved from possible death by a man intensely dedicated to performing what he felt to be his duty. In that brief instant, in the midst of war, he had envisioned his chief responsibility to be that of a Christian and a man of charity. It is only by recognizing this devotion to duty that one can understand how a man who, according to one biographer, took the Indian boy in his arms, dissolved some brown sugar in water and coaxed him to drink, could in 1835 turn a deaf ear to the heart-rending appeals of John Ross to save the Cherokees from the destruction of their lives and homes.[65]

When in 1835 a minority splinter group of Cherokees signed away all the nation's lands in the Treaty of New Echota, Jackson's great objective was achieved.[66] In his Seventh Annual Message, on December 7, 1835, Jackson wrote at great length of the extent and richness of the land which the Indians were to receive, the guarantees of their permanent occupancy of the territory and plans for their protection and improvement. It was an optimistic address. No mention was made of the possible extinction of the race. The verbal picture was one of the Indians living in a land of milk and honey, prospering, and gradually, with the aid of the government, turning to the civilized pursuits of agriculture and mechanics. These were the *right* sentiments to express at the time. They were the words of a benevolent conqueror. The President even acknowledged that we

[63] *Ibid.*, 215-16 (December 7, 1823).
[64] Marquis James, *Andrew Jackson: Portrait of a President*, 160. There is no reference to Lyncoya's death among the published writings of Jackson. Strangely enough, most of his other biographers fail to make mention of the youth.
[65] James Parton, *Life of Andrew Jackson*, I, 368; Bassett, *Correspondence*, V, 319-20, From John Ross (January 13, 1835).
[66] Jackson submitted the treaty to the Senate on March 5, 1836; Richardson, *Messages*, III, 225. For a discussion of the negotiations see Harmon, *Sixty Years*, 189-90.

owed a "moral debt" to the Indians, a large part of which would be paid by the grants stipulated in the treaty.[67]

It is impossible to determine whether Jackson really believed that the glorious picture he presented would become a reality. From past evidence, it appears that his primary concern in voicing such sentiments was to placate those who heard them. With the battle over, Jackson was probably intent upon soothing the wounds of his opponents, rather than worrying about any long range program of rehabilitation.

Jackson spoke of the long history of the Indian problem being consummated as a result of the Cherokee treaty. In this he was wrong as all the treaty-makers who had preceded him. The results of the negotiations at New Echota put a period to the problem in Georgia as King Philip's War had closed it in Massachusetts. Only five months after Jackson left the White House, news of a Seminole uprising in Florida reached The Hermitage, and Old Hickory's reaction was true to form. "A well chosen brigade with such officers as I could select, numbering a thousand bayonets and rifles, in addition to the regulars now in Florida, would destroy the Seminole Indians in 30 days. . . . Powell [half breed leader of the Seminoles] . . . ought to have been hung or kept in irons. . . ." [68]

The important points of difference between Jackson's approach to the Indian problem and those of the Presidents who preceded him lay in his intense devotion to the cause of removing the Indian threat and the relentless vigor with which he pursued his objectives. He was aided by a refusal to allow emotionalism to stand in his way and a readiness to circumvent legal hurdles like the treaty-making process and the decisions of the Supreme Court. It is interesting to note that one of Jackson's last references to the Indians was contained in a confidential letter to Francis P. Blair, in which he expressed annoyance "that the Secretary of War should be inveigled by John Ross and the enemies of the administration into the measure of prolonging their [Cherokees] stay within the state". Such a step, he stated, "is the most astonishing thing that has ever happened, and shows that the secretary of war is half an age behind the times in our Indian affairs".[69]

---

[67] Richardson, *Messages,* III, 171-72.
[68] Bassett, *Correspondence,* V, 507, To the Secretary of War (Joel R. Poinsett) (August 27, 1837).
[69] *Ibid.,* 553 (June 4, 1838).

Jackson might have said that the Secretary of War had retrogressed to the days of President John Quincy Adams, when consideration for the opinions and rights of the Indians was allowed to impede the forward progress of white man's greed. However, events proved that Jackson had little to fear; the Cherokees were removed, and Martin Van Buren was given the unenviable credit for carrying to completion Jackson's Indian policy in the "Trail of Tears".

The Cherokee removal was undoubtedly one of the most ignoble deeds to be found on the pages of our history. Since the act was a direct result of Andrew Jackson's Indian policy, he has rightfully borne the brunt of the criticism. However, if Jackson is today considered unique among the Presidents in the methods he employed in dealing with the red men, there was nothing particularly unique in the motives for his policy. The other two Presidents given major attention in this study shared Jackson's belief that the savage Indian and the civilized white could not live side by side. The terms for Indian existence outlined by both Adams and Jefferson were clearly those of the white man, primarily serving the white man's material well-being and physical safety. Though Jackson did not exhibit a scientific interest in the Indians or a deep concern for their lot, there is no evidence that he was stained by any hatred for them as a race. Rather, like the Negroes, they were viewed as being outside the mainstream of American life, to be treated in a manner which would best serve the immediate interests of national growth, unity and safety.

CHAPTER VII

A FOCAL VIEW

The three great leaders given major attention in this work differed from one another in the nature and intensity of their views toward the Negro and Indian and the problems they represented. This was not unusual, considering the differences in the backgrounds of these men and their varied personal experiences with the colored races. Thus John Adams from mercantile Massachusetts, whose contacts with Negroes had been rare and to whom the Indian was little more than a legend, understandably displayed no great interest in the color problem. Thus Thomas Jefferson, whose status as slave owner had been inherited rather than sought after and whose personal contacts with Indians had been under conditions which would inspire poets and scholars, could express a desire to lighten their burden. And thus Andrew Jackson, whose slaves had been acquired during the years of his struggle up the social and economic ladder and were a mark of his success, and to whom Indians had most often represented political and military impediments, could illustrate a wholly pragmatic attitude in his dealings with these races.

Despite these personal differences, however, when as national political figures the three men were faced with the color problem, their ultimate policies were basically the same. Neither President Adams, whose distaste for slavery had been for the most part restricted to his personal life, nor President Jefferson, who in his younger days appeared ready to lead an anti-slavery crusade, can be credited with presenting a program to lighten the Negroes' burdens one iota. Though there were some differences in the intensity and sincerity with which the three men called for and inaugurated plans to civilize the Indians, the government's policy of neutralizing the military threat of the red man and obtaining his hunting lands was faithfully pursued by each. The policy of Indian removal was advocated by the humanitarian Jefferson and made national policy by Jackson, the Indian fighter.

The fact that there was a government Indian policy whereas none existed for the Negro, apart from the decisions regarding the African slave trade, can be attributed in part to the constitutional divisions of responsibility and power between state and federal governments. However, these divisions came into play only after territories became states. Why was the Indian story the same in territory after territory? Why was there no similar consistency regarding Negro slavery? The answers lay to some extent in the men who guided our nation, but the roots were in the people whence these men sprang and whose representatives they were.

For a brief instant the enlightened spirit of the Revolution had brought with it a revulsion against slavery. But the light glimmered briefly and faded from view, leaving only a fairly high degree of unanimity regarding the immorality of the external slave trade. This was the only aspect of slavery which the three men saw fit to condemn when they played upon the national stage. Over the years following the Revolution the spirit of the Enlightenment, so well expressed by the younger Jefferson, appears to have been affected to some extent by a spirit of pragmatism, so obvious in the deeds of Andrew Jackson. The result was an attitude of doing what was of most immediate importance and what could be accomplished with the least amount of dissension. Abolishing the external slave trade was an example of the latter, welding national unity an example of the former.

National unity was the most important cause and the most significant driving force behind the policies of the three Presidents. The slavery question was a divisive issue. Each of them recognized it as such and, having a desire to see the nation grow and prosper, each at one time or another acted in such a way as to discourage its entry into the political limelight. However, Adams, Jefferson and Jackson did not by any stretch of the imagination avoid all divisive issues. Devotion to a set of broad goals for the United States united these men into the category of patriotic leaders; the different means they advocated divided them and sent them into different political parties. The combination of patriotism and political awareness which caused them to avoid slavery as a major national issue led them at times to utilize it as a secondary lever in the attainment of what was to them a more important goal and one which appeared possible of achieving.

Since they themselves had used the slavery issue to achieve political advantage, it was not surprising that Jefferson and Jackson interpreted the early stirrings of northern based anti-slavery agitation and the more vocal defense of the system emanating from the South as the work of political opportunists. This is not meant to imply that our national heroes were hypocrits. Their antagonism toward the *vocal* and *public* entry of the issue into national affairs absolves them from such a charge. The fact that in all three cases opposition was based primarily upon the threat the agitators posed to the national interest and safety and to political unity, rather than to the existence of slavery itself, strengthens their positions as men devoted to the Union.

A question arises, however, as to the relationship between personal convictions and political leadership. We have seen that both Adams and Jefferson, who were antagonistic to slavery, not only failed to attempt to create public support for their position but in fact seem to have sacrificed their convictions to attain other goals. In order to stress the importance of a land-owning aristocracy to the stability of the nation, Adams could ask John Taylor of Caroline to imagine the devastating effects upon the South of a sudden Congressional act freeing all the slaves. Thomas Jefferson could reverse his position on the diffusion of slavery when the Missouri crisis threatened to split the Union. Thus it appears that devotion to a cause is just one aspect determining the position taken by a political leader. Equally significant is its relative importance when compared with other causes and the degree of support that can be expected from the people. As much as Jefferson indicated a desire to see slavery eliminated, he did not move much faster than his fellow Southerners in the areas of either political or social reform of the institution. Such an attitude was not limited to Jefferson or to anti-slavery activities. It can be observed in Jackson's hesitancy to push the Texas issue at a time when he knew that majority support was doubtful and that the Union and the Democratic Party might be endangered by such action.

These men reflected and gave direction to public opinion, rather than attempting to create or convert the people to a cause. One reason history has separated them from the mass is that they appear to have been one step ahead of the rest in thoughts or deeds or both. However, if the left foot was planted in front of the ranks of the populace, the right foot, trailing behind, identified from where they came — from the state, the nation, the party, the class. None of these cried out to be led in a battle against slavery, a fact all three men appear to have been well aware of by the time they achieved the Presidency. Thus the personal convictions and inconsistencies regarding the Negro problem, discernible in their private correspondence, did not appear in their public statements, nor were they reflected in their public policies.

It is impossible to describe in simple terms a general American attitude toward the Indian. As has been seen, it was possible for a single individual to view him with a mixture of admiration, awe, sympathy and fear, to advocate at one time a policy to ameliorate his conditions and perpetuate his race, and at another time to call for his destruction or removal. There appears to have existed a noble savage concept of the Indian, with emphasis on the noble by those who had the least personal contact with him and during times of relative peace on the frontier, and emphasis on the savage by those who lived closest to his village and during times of war or periods when the pressure for westward expansion was greatest. Despite the apparent differences in their actual concern for the Indian, it seems as if every peace-time public reference to him by the Presidents contained gestures of good will and kind intentions. There was also general agreement among the Chief Executives that the soil must serve the interests of the civilized white man. And so, with gestures of good will, the Indian was ultimately shoved further and further into the wilderness. This was clearly what the West demanded and what the other sections were either willing to see happen or about which they were not interested enough to act. For, with the exception of the ugly incidents of the Cherokee removal, the policy evoked no opposition from large sectors of the populace. The romantic tales of James Fenimore Cooper apparently held more interest for the people of the East and Indian-free sections of the South than the ugly realities of functioning Indian policy.

It does not take a great deal of imagination to recognize that much of the present-day attitude toward the color problem reflects that of the early national period. The Indian warrior of old captures the romantic fancy of our sculptors, painters, movie makers and promoters of rodeos, while the problems of the Indian today go largely unheeded. The public finds amusement in the stories of the few Indians who have "struck it rich" on Oklahoma oil, but there are few voices raised to demand alleviation of the conditions on the reservations in the Southwest. The Negro problem today is far more complex than that which faced Adams, Jefferson and Jackson, and, unlike those men, today's Presidents cannot avoid facing the issue on the public forum. But the realization of the divisive danger engendered by this problem has been as evident in the policies of the twentieth century as it was in those of the early national period. Political reality can be as effective a brake now as it was then.

There is still another legacy from the past which hovers about the color problem today, that of color pigmentation itself. The willingness of Jefferson and others to accept the possibility of the amalgamation of the red and white races was not extended to the black. Jefferson clearly stated his repugnance for the Negro's physiognomy, and even Benjamin Rush could not foresee any manner of mixture of the races until the Negro turned white. Though Andrew Jackson did not comment upon the racial characteristics of the Negroes, it would be difficult to visualize his adopting a Negro into his intimate family life in the manner followed with the Indian boy Lyncoya. The relatively easy degree of acceptance in Jackson's day of an Indian-white marriage compared with the social ostracism facing a similar union of white and black also carriers over into the social attitudes of our own era. Though the scientific reasoning in Jefferson's writings was at fault, he was rather accurate in visualizing the future problems of freed Negroes within the United States as involving physical as well as cultural obstacles, while stressing only the latter as the primary impediment for the Indians.

The early national period was one in which a large measure of the future destiny of our political system was shaped. It is understandable that the authors of survey texts have emphasized those events of the era which marked the formation of the party system, the establishment of the judicial process and the relationship between state and federal governments. However, the Negro problem, which draws the major textbook attention in studying the eighteen-fifties, and the Indian problem, which is usually given its major treatment in the post-Reconstruction chapters, were very much present in these early decades of our national history. No knowledge of what was can be very penetrating without prefatory understanding of what had been.

The silence of Adams, the dilemmas of Jefferson and the pragmatism of Jackson are as much a part of the story as the colorful events surrounding the generations of leaders who were to follow.

BIBLIOGRAPHY

PRIMARY SOURCES

Collected Writings

Adams, Charles Francis (ed.), *Familiar Letters of John Adams and His Wife, Abigail Adams, During the Revolution* (New York, Houghton Mifflin Company, 1875).

——, *Letters of John Adams Addressed to His Wife,* 2 vols. (Boston, C. C. Little and J. Brown, 1841).

——, *The Works of John Adams,* 10 vols. (Boston, Little, Brown and Company, 1856).

Bassett, John Spencer (ed.), *Correspondence of Andrew Jackson,* 7 vols. (Washington, D.C., Carnegie Institution of Washington, 1926-1935).

Bergh, Albert Ellery (ed.), *The Writings of Thomas Jefferson,* 20 vols. (Washington, D.C., The Thomas Jefferson Memorial Association, 1907).

Blount, William, *The Blount Journal, 1790-1796* (Nashville, Tennessee Historical Commission, 1955).

Bowers, Claude G. (ed.), *The Diary of Elbridge Gerry, Jr.* (New York, Brentano's, 1927).

Boyd, Julan P. (ed.), *The Papers of Thomas Jefferson,* 17 vols. (Princeton, New Jersey, Princeton University Press, 1952-1965).

Briant, Lemuel, *The Absurdity of Blasphemy* (Boston, Green, 1750).

——, *Some More Friendly Remarks* (Boston, Green, 1750).

——, *Some More Friendly Remarks* (Boston, Green, 1751).

Burnett, Edmund Cody (ed.), *Letters of Members of the Continental Congress,* 8 vols. (Washington, D.C., The Carnegie Institution of Washington, 1921-1936).

Butterfield, L. H. (ed.), *Adams Family Correspondence,* 2 vols. (Cambridge, The Belknap Press of Harvard University Press, 1963).

——, *Diary and Autobiography of John Adams,* 4 vols. (Cambridge, The Belknap Press of Harvard University Press, 1961).

Cappon, Lester J. (ed.), *The Adams-Jefferson Letters,* 2 vols. (Chapel Hill, The University of North Carolina Press, 1959).

Ford, Paul Leicester (ed.), *The Works of Thomas Jefferson,* 10 vols. (New York, G. P. Putnam's Sons, 1892-1899).

Ford, Worthington Chauncey (ed.), *Statesman and Friend: Correspondence of John Adams with Benjamin Waterhouse, 1784-1822* (Boston, Little, Brown and Company, 1927).

Hamilton, J. G. Rothau (ed.), *The Best Letters of Thomas Jefferson* (Boston, Houghton Mifflin Company, 1926).

Jefferson, Thomas, *Notes on the State of Virginia* (Chapel Hill, University of North Carolina Press, 1955) (first printed in 1785).

Mullet, Charles F. (ed.), *Some Political Writings of James Otis,* 2 vols. (Columbia, Missouri, University of Missouri Press, 1929).

Richardson, James D. (ed.), *A Compilation of the Messages and Papers of the Presidents, 1789-1897,* 10 vols. (Washington, D.C., Published by authority of Congress, 1898).

Warren-Adams Letters, 2 vols. (Boston, Massachusetts Historical Society, 1917).

Washington, H. A. (ed.), *The Writings of Thomas Jefferson,* 9 vols. (Washington, D.C., Taylor and Maury, 1853).

Wilstach, Paul (ed.), *Correspondence of John Adams and Thomas Jefferson, 1812-1826* (Indianapolis, The Bobbs-Merrill Company, 1925).

Memoirs and Personal Accounts

Eaton, John, *The Life of Andrew Jackson Major-General in the Service of United States: Comprising a History of the War in the South from the Commencement of the Creek Campaign to the Termination of Hostilities Before New Orleans* (Philadelphia, Samuel F. Bradford, 1824).

Isaac, *Memoirs of a Monticello Slave* (as dictated to Charles Campbell) (Charlotteville, University of Virginia Press, 1951).

Quincy, Josiah, *Figures of the Past* (Boston, Little, Brown and Company, 1870).

Sparks, W. H., *The Memories of Fifty Years* (Philadelphia, E. Claxton and Company, 1870).

Records, Documents and Reports

American State Papers, Indian Affairs, 2 vols. (Washington, Gales and Seaton, 1832-1834).

Bates, Samuel (ed.), *Records of the Town of Braintree, 1640-1793* (Randolph, Massachusetts, Daniel H. Husford, 1886).

Commager, Henry Steele (ed.), *Documents of American History,* Seventh edition (New York, Appleton-Century-Crofts, Inc., 1963).

Debates of the Convention of the Commonwealth of Massachusetts Convened at Boston at the 9th of January, 1788, and Continued until the 7th of February for the Purpose of Asserting to and Ratifying the Constitution Recommended by the Grand Federal Convention (Boston, Olive and Monroe and Joshua Cushing, 1808).

Department of Commerce and Labor, Bureau of the Census, *A Century of Population Growth, 1790-1900* (Washington, D.C., Government Printing Office, 1909).

Journal of the House of Representatives of Massachusetts, 1723-1724, vol. 5 (Boston, Massachusetts Historical Society, 1924).

United States Department of State, *The Diplomatic Correspondence of the United States of America, 1783-1789,* 7 vols. (Washington, D.C., F. P. Blair, 1833-1834).

SECONDARY SOURCES

State and Local Histories

Abernathy, Thomas Perkins, *From Frontier to Plantation in Tennessee* (Chapel Hill, The University of North Carolina Press, 1932).

Andrews, Mathew Page, *Virginia, The Old Dominion* (Garden City, New York, Doubleday, Doran and Company, Inc., 1937).

Arnold, Marian Sophie (ed.), *A Brief History of the Town of Braintree* (Boston, Thomas Todd Company, 1940).

Austin, George Lowell, *The History of Massachusetts from the Landing of the Pilgrims to the Present Time* (Boston, Rand, Avery and Company, 1884).

Brown, Robert E., *Middle-Class Democracy and the Revolution in Massachusetts, 1691-1780* (Ithaca, Cornell University Press, 1955).

Folmsbee, Stanley J., Robert E. Corlew, and Enoch L. Mitchell, *History of Tennessee*, 4 vols. (New York, Lewis Historical Publishing Company, 1960).

Hale, William Thomas and Dixon L. Merritt, *A History of Tennessee and Tennesseans*, 8 vols. (Chicago, The Lewis Publishing Company, 1913).

Harner, Philip Max (ed.), *Tennessee: A Hisory, 1673-1932*, 4 vols. (New York, The American Historical Society, Inc., 1933).

Hart, Albert Bushnell (ed.), *Commonwealth History of Massachusetts*, 5 vols. (New York, The State History Company, 1927-1928).

Hemphill, William Edwin, Marvin Wilson Schlegal and Sadie Ethel Engelberg, *Cavalier Commonwealth: History and Government of Virginia* (New York, McGraw-Hill Book Company, 1957).

Kellaway, William, *The New England Company, 1649-1776* (New York, Barnes and Noble, Inc., 1961).

Moore, John Trotwood and Austin P. Foster (eds.), *Tennessee, The Volunteer State, 1769-1923*, 4 vols. (Chicago, The S. J. Clark Publishing Company, 1923).

Pattee, William S. A., *A History of Old Braintree and Quincy* (Quincy, Massachusetts, Green and Prescott, 1878).

Wertenbaker, Thomas Jefferson, *The Planters of Colonial Virginia* (Princeton, Princeton University Press, 1922).

Wilson, Daniel Munro, *Where American Independence Began: Quincy, Its Famous Group of Patriots, Their Deeds, Homes and Descendants* (Boston, Houghton Mifflin and Company, 1902).

Church History

Bacon, Leonard W., *The Story of the Churches: The Congregationalist* (New York, The Baker and Taylor Company, 1904).

Biographies

Bassett, John Spencer, *The Life of Andrew Jackson* (New York, The Macmillan Company, 1928).

Beloff, Max, *Thomas Jefferson and American Democracy* (New York, Collier Books, 1962).

Bemis, Samuel Flagg, *John Quincy Adams and the Foundations of American Foreign Policy* (New York, Alfred A. Knopf, 1949).

——, *John Quincy Adams and the Union* (New York, Alfred A. Knopf, 1956).

Boorstin, Daniel J., *The Lost World of Thomas Jefferson* (New York, Henry Holt and Company, 1948).

Bowen, Catherine Drinker, *John Adams and the American Revolution* (Boston, Little, Brown and Company, 1950).

Brant, Irving, *James Madison, Commander in Chief, 1812-1836* (Indianapolis, The Bobbs-Merrill Company, 1961).

——, *James Madison, Father of the Constitution, 1787-1800* (Indianapolis, The Bobbs-Merrill Company, 1950).

——, *James Madison, The Nationalist, 1780-1787* (Indianapolis, The Bobbs-Merrill Company, 1948).

——, *James Madison, The President, 1809-1812 (Indianapolis,* The Bobbs-Merrill Company, 1956).

——, *James Madison, Secretary of State, 1800-1809* (Indianapolis, The Bobbs-Merrill Company, 1953).

——, *James Madison, The Virginia Revolutionist* (Indianapolis, The Bobbs-Merrill Company, 1941).

Burke, Pauline Wilcox, *Emily Donelson of Tennessee*, 2 vols. (Richmond, Virginia, Garrett and Massie, 1941).

Burns, Edward McNall, *James Madison, Philosopher of the Constitution* (New Brunswick, Rutgers University Press, 1938).

Chinard, Gilbert, *Honest John Adams* (Boston, Little, Brown and Company, 1933).

——, *Thomas Jefferson, The Apostle of Americanism* (Boston, Little, Brown and Company, 1943).

Correa, Moylan Walsh, *The Political Science of John Adams* (New York, G. P. Putnam's Sons, 1915).

Cresson, W. P., *James Monroe* (Chapel Hill, University of North Carolina Press, 1946).

Dos Passos, John, *The Head and Heart of Thomas Jefferson* (Garden City, New York, Doubleday and Company, Inc., 1954).

Erney, Richard Alton, "The Public Life of Henry Dearborn", Unpublished Ph. D. thesis. Teachers College, Columbia University, New York, 1957.

Gay, Sydney Howard, *James Madison* (Boston, Houghton Mifflin Company, 1892).

Gilman, Daniel C., *James Monroe* (Boston, Houghton Mifflin Company, 1899).

Haraszti, Zoltan, *John Adams and the Prophets of Progress* (Cambridge, Harvard University Press, 1952).

Hunt, Gaillard, *The Life of James Madison* (New York, Doubleday, Page and Company, 1902).

James, Marquis, *Andrew Jackson, The Border Captain* (Indianapolis, The Bobbs-Merrill Company, 1933).

——, *Andrew Jackson: Portrait of a President* (Indianapolis, The Bobbs-Merrill Company, 1940).

Koch, Adrienne, *The Philosophy of Thomas Jefferson* (New York, Columbia University Press, 1943).

McCormac, Eugene Irving, *James K. Polk: A Political Biography* (Berkeley, The University of California Press, 1922).

McCory, Charles A., *Polk and the Presidency* (Austin, University of Texas Press, 1960).

McCoy, Samuel, *This Man Adams* (New York, Brentano's, 1928).

Malone, Dumas, *Jefferson and the Ordeal of Liberty* (Boston, Little, Brown and Company, 1962).

——, *Jefferson and the Rights of Man* (Boston, Little, Brown and Company, 1951).

——, *Jefferson the Virginian* (Boston, Little, Brown and Company, 1948).

Mayo, Bernard, *Jefferson Himself* (Boston, Houghton Mifflin Company, 1942).

Morgan, George, *The Life of James Monroe* (Boston, Small, Maynard and Company, 1921).

Morrel, Martha McBuck, *"Young Hickory": The Life and Times of President James K. Polk* (New York, E. P. Dutton and Company, Inc., 1949).

Morse, John T., Jr., *John Adams* (Boston, Houghton Mifflin Company, 1896).

Padover, Saul K., *Jefferson* (New York, Harcourt, Brace and Company, 1942).
—, *A Jefferson Profile As Revealed in His Letters* (New York, The John Day Company, 1956).
Parton, James, *Life of Andrew Jackson*, 3 vols. (New York, Mason Brothers, 1860).
—, *Life of Thomas Jefferson, Third President of the United States* (Boston, J. R. Osgood and Company, 1874).
Prentiss, Henry Putnam, *Timothy Pickering as the Leader of New England Federalism, 1800-1815* (Evanston, Northwestern University Press, 1932).
Randall, Henry Stephens, *The Life of Thomas Jefferson*, 3 vols. (Philadelphia, J. P. Lippincott Company, 1888).
Remini, Robert V., *Martin Van Buren and the Making of the Democratic Party* (New York, Columbia University Press, 1959).
Sellers, Charles Grier, Jr., *James K. Polk, Jacksonian* (Princeton, Princeton University Press, 1957).
Shepard, Edward M., *Martin Van Buren* (Boston, Houghton Mifflin Company, 1888).
Smith, Abbot Emerson, *James Madison, Builder* (New York, Wilson-Erickson, Inc., 1937).
Smith, Page, *John Adams*, 2 vols. (Garden City, New York, Doubleday and Company, Inc., 1962).
Styron, Arthur, *The Last of the Cocked Hats: James Monroe and the Virginia Dynasty* (Norman, University of Oklahoma Press, 1945).
Ward, John William, *Andrew Jackson, Symbol for an Age* (New York, Oxford University Press, 1955).

Works Concerned with the Jeffersonian and Jacksonian Heritages

Adams, James Truslow, *The Living Jefferson* (New York, Charles Scribner's Sons, 1936).
Peterson, Merril D., *The Jefferson Image in the American Mind* (New York, Oxford University Press, 1960).
Syrett, Howard Coffin, *Andrew Jackson: His Contribution to the American Tradition* (Indianapolis, The Bobbs-Merril Company, 1953).
Wiltse, Charles Maurice, *The Jeffersonian Tradition in American Democracy* (Chapel Hill, University of North Carolina Press, 1935).

Monographs Dealing with Party Politics and Presidential Administrations

Bowers, Claude G., *The Party Battles of the Jackson Period* (Boston, Houghton Mifflin Company, 1922).
Dangerfield, George, *The Era of Good Feelings* (London, Methuen and Company, Ltd., 1953).
Dauer, Manning J., *The Adams Federalists* (Baltimore, The Johns Hopkins Press, 1953).
Hofstadter, Richard, *The American Political Tradition* (New York, Alfred A. Knopf, Inc., 1948).
Kurtz, Stephen G., *The Presidency of John Adams* (Philadelphia, University of Pennsylvania Press, 1957).
Meyers, Marvin, *The Jacksonian Persuasion* (Stanford, Stanford University Press, 1957).
Schlesinger, Arthur M., Jr., *The Age of Jackson* (Boston, Little, Brown and Company, 1945).

Van Deusen, Glyndon G., *The Jacksonian Era, 1828-1848* (New York, Harper and Brothers, 1959).
White, Leonard D., *The Federalists: A Study in Administrative History* (New York, The Macmillan Company, 1948).
——, *The Jacksonians: A Study in Administrative History, 1829-1861* (New York, The Macmillan Company, 1954).
——, *The Jeffersonians: A Study in Administrative History, 1801-1829* (New York, The Macmillan Company, 1951).

Works Concerned with the Negro and Slavery

Davis, David Brian, *The Problem of Slavery in Western Culture* (Ithaca, N.Y., Cornell University Press, 1966).
Dumond, Dwight Lowell, *Antislavery: The Crusade for Freedom in America* (Ann Arbor, The University of Michigan Press, 1961).
Durham, John Stephens, *To Teach the Negro History* (Philadelphia, David McKay Publisher, 1897).
Franklin, John Hope, *From Slavery to Freedom* (New York, Alfred A. Knopf, 1956).
Gossett, Thomas F., *Race, The History of an Idea in America* (Dallas, Southern Methodist University Press, 1963).
Greene, Lorenzo Johnston, *The Negro in Colonial New England, 1620-1776* (New York, Columbia University Press, 1942).
Logan, Rayford W., *The Negro in the United States* (Princeton, New Jersey, D. Van Nostrand Company, Inc., 1957).
McColley, Robert, *Slavery and Jeffersonian Virginia* (Urbana, University of Illinois Press, 1965).
Mellon, Mathew T., *Early American Views on Negro Slavery* (Boston, Meador Publishing Company, 1934).
Myrdal, Gunnar, *An American Dilemma: The Negro Problem and Modern Democracy*, 2 vols. (New York, Harper and Brothers Publishers, 1944).
Ottley, Roi, *Black Odyssey: The Story of the Negro in America* (New York, Charles Scribner's Sons, 1948).
Phillips, Ulrich B., *American Negro Slavery* (New York, D. Appleton and Company, 1926).
Stanton, William, *The Leopard's Spots: Scientific Attitudes Toward Race in America, 1815-1859* (Chicago, The University of Chicago Press, 1960).
Weyl, Nathaniel, *The Negro in American Civilization* (Washington, D.C., Public Affairs Press, 1960).
Woodson, Carter G., *The Negro in Our History* (Washington, D.C., The Associated Publishers, Inc., 1941).

Works Concerned with the Indian

Gossett, Thomas F., *Race, The History of an Idea in America* (Dallas, Southern Methodist University Press, 1963).
Hagan, William T., *American Indians* (Chicago, The University of Chicago Press, 1961).
Hamilton, Charles Everett, *Cry of the Thunderbird: The American Indian's Own Story* (New York, The Macmillan Company, 1950).
Harmon, George D., *Sixty Years of Indian Affairs; Political, Economic and Diplomatic: 1789-1850.* (Chapel Hill, The University of North Carolina Press, 1941).

Josephy, Alvin M., Jr. (ed.), *The American Heritage Book of Indians* (Washington, D.C., American Heritage Publishing Company, Inc., 1961).

Keiser, Albert, *The Indian in American Literature* (New York, Oxford University Press, 1933).

Lauber, Almon Wheeler, *Indian Slavery in Colonial Times Within the Present Limits of the United States* (New York, Columbia University, 1913).

Macleod, William C., *The American Indian Frontier* (New York, Alfred A. Knopf, 1928).

McNickle, D'Arcy, *They Came Here First: The Epic of the American Indian* (Philadelphia, J. P. Lippincott Company, 1949).

Pearce, Roy Harvey, *The Savages of America: A Study of the Indian and the Idea of Civilization* (Baltimore, The Johns Hopkins Press, 1953).

Prucha, Francis Paul, *American Indian Policy in the Formative Years: The Indian Trade and Intercourse Acts, 1790-1834* (Cambridge, Harvard University Press, 1962).

Stanton, William, *The Leopard's Spots: Scientific Attitudes Toward Race in America, 1815-1859* (Chicago, The University of Chicago Press, 1960).

Washburn, Wilcomb E. (ed.), *The Indian and the White Man* (New York, New York University Press, 1964).

Wissler, Clark, *Indians of the United States* (New York, Doubleday, Doran and Company, Inc., 1949).

Woodward, Grace Steele, *The Cherokees* (Norman, The University of Oklahoma Press, 1963).

Periodicals

Chamberlain, Alxander F., "Thomas Jefferson's Ethnological Opinions and Activities", *American Anthropologist*, IX (July, 1907), 499-509.

Farrison, W. Edward, "The Origin of Brown's *Clotel*", *Phylon*, XV (December, 1954), 347-354.

Graham, Pearl M., "Thomas Jefferson and Sally Hemming", *Journal of Negro History*, XLVI (April, 1961), 89-103.

Greene, John C., "Some Early Speculations on the Origin of Human Races", *American Anthropologist*, LVI (February, 1954), 31-41.

Howe, John R., Jr., "John Adam's Views of Slavery", *Journal of Negro History*, XLIX (July, 1964), 201-206.

Merk, Frederick, "A Safety Valve Thesis and Texas Annexation", *The Mississippi Valley Historical Review*, XLIX (December, 1962), 413-436.

"Thomas Jefferson's Thoughts on the Negro", *Journal of Negro History*, III (January, 1918), 55-89.

INDEX

Adams, Abigail, on Negro slavery, 25, 26

Adams, John, 48, 69, 82, 85, 112, 113, 150

——, place in history, 11

——, author of *A Defense of the Constitution of the Government of the United States of America*, 34

——, author of *Discourses on Davila*, 35

——, church membership of, 25

——, legal practice of, 12, 13

——, delegate to Continental Congress, 13-15, 21

——, at The Hague, 34

——, at Paris peace negotiations, 15, 16, 33

——, as minister to Great Britain, 15, 16, 34

——, as Vice President, 34

——, as President, 19, 35, 37-39, 41-42

——, political associates of, 28, 45-46

——, on Indians, 11, 19, 32-47, 62, 156, 157; on civilizing Indians, 37, 41, 42, 47; on converting Indians to Christianity, 41, 47; encounters with Indians, 32, 33, 42; on govt. Indian policy, 35-37, 39-40, 156; on Indian culture, 34, 35, 38, 39, 41, 42, 45; on Indian origins, 38, 39; on nature of Indian warfare, 32-33, 40; on racial attributes of Indians, 38, 45

——, on Negroes and slavery, 11-31, 45, 157; on abolition, 17, 21; compares conditions of slaves with free labor, 15, 18; on emancipation, 15, 19, 20, 26, 159; encounters with Negroes, 11-13, 20, 21, 25, 157; on legislation concerning Negroes, slavery and the slave trade, 15-17, 19-20; on Missouri crisis, 19; on Negro racial attributes, 11, 12-13, 21; on Negro slavery in Maryland, 17, 21; on Negro slavery in West Indies, 12; on Negro slaves carried off by British troops during Revolution, 16; on slave holders, 12, 17, 18, 20, 21; on slave insurrections, 18; on slave trade, 15, 17; on slavery views in *Notes on the State of Va.*, 16; views slavery as a divisive political issue, 15-16, 19-20.

Adams, John Quincy, 11, 21, 129

——, on American Colonization Society, 30

——, on Indians, 46-47, 145, 156

——, on Negro slavery, 29-31; on slave trade, 29

Africa, as possible receiver of American Negroes, 54, 68, 71; slave trade in, 17, 51, 158

Alabama, encroachments on Indian lands by, 147

American Colonization Society, J. Q. Adams on, 30; James Madison on, 78

American Philosophical Society, 74, 89, 90 n.

Anti-Slavery Society, 30

Bacon, Leonard, church historian, cited, 23

Balch, Alfred, 147

Bancroft, Edward, 61

Banneker, Benjamin, 72, 73

Barbary pirates, 17

Barbour, James, 46

Barlow, Joel, 72, 73 n.

Barton, Benjamin, 75, 80, 83 n., 84, 89

Benton, Thomas Hart, 133 n.

Blair, Francis P., 133 n., 134, 155

Blount, Willie, 136, 138

Boorstin, Daniel, author of *The Lost*

86, 89-90, 93, 99, 114; on Indian
racial attributes, 85-89, 105; on
nature of Indian warfare, 85, 113
——, on mullatoes, 53, 54
——, on Negroes and slavery, 48-81,
91, 159; on abolition, 51, 61, 67,
159; on emancipation, 50, 52, 54,
58-62, 66-68, 70-72, 77, 80, 81;
on expansion of slavery, 53, 54, 63,
69-70, 159; on freed Negroes, 52-
54, 62, 64, 68, 70-71, 91; on freed
Negroes, colonization of, 55, 64,
67, 68, 70, 71; on legislative acts
concerning Negroes, slavery, and
slave trade, 52-55, 65, 66, 68, 69;
on Missouri crisis, 70, 159; on Negro racial attributes, 55-58, 63, 72-
74, 80, 81, 88, 161; on runaway
slaves, 61, 62; on slaveholders, 55,
58, 68, 80; as slave master, 48-50,
61, 62, 66; on slave revolts, 62-64,
80; on slave trade, 50-52, 65-66,
68, 91; on slavery as a divisive
political issue, 59-61, 67-70, 80; on
slavery in Greece and Rome, 58;
on treatment of slaves, 49, 54, 61,
63, 68-69; on Phyllis Wheatley and
Ignatio Sancho, 57
Jeffersonian Republicans, 18
Johnson's *Wonder Working Provi-
dences,* cited, 42-43

Kaskaskia Indians, 105
Kendall, Amos, 131
King Philip's War, 42-45, 155
King, Rufus, 65
Knox, Henry, 95

Ledyard, John, 83, 84, 93
Lee, Thomas, 53
Lewis, Meriwether, 108, 109, 110 n.
Lewis, Nicholas, 50
Lewis, William B., 134
Lindley, Jacob, 18, 19, 21
Livingston, Robert, 16
Lloyd, James, 37
Logan, Dr. George, 67
Louisiana, Negro slavery in, 28, 29,
68
Lyle, James, 62
Lyman, Theodore, Jr., 30
Lyncoya, Indian boy adopted by An-
drew Jackson, 153-54, 161
McKee, John, 136, 137

Madison, James, 54 n., 59, 60, 68, 83,
111, 114 n., 140
——, on Indians, 116-19
——, on Negroes, slavery and slave
trade, 76-78, 80
Madison, Reverend James, 74
Maryland, Negro slavery in, 17, 21
Mason, George, 53
Massachusetts, 13, 14, 30, 157
——, freed Negroes in, 22-24
——, Indians in, 23, 41-45, 47
——, mulattoes in, 23
——, Negro slavery in, 15, 22-24, 26-
28, 47; legislative acts regarding
Negroes, slavery and slave trade,
15, 22-24, 26
Mather, Cotton, 23
Mayo, Bernard, author of *Jefferson
Himself,* cited, 71-72
Merryweather, David, 129, 140
Missouri Crisis, 68
——, John Adams on, 19; John Quin-
cy Adams on, 30; Andrew Jackson
on, 129; Thomas Jefferson on, 69-
70, 159; James Madison on, 78;
James Monroe on, 79
Mitchell, David B., 128, 129, 129 n.
Mohawk Indians, 36, 116
Monroe, James, 63, 64, 70, 96, 113,
114, 127, 128, 140-42, 153
——, on Indians, 117-19, 143, 145,
145 n.
——, on Negroes, slavery, and slave
trade, 78-80
Monticello, 48-50, 61, 66
Morse, Jedidiah, 113-14
Mulattoes, in Boston, Mass., 24
——, Thomas Jefferson on, 53, 54
——, in Massachusetts, 23

Negroes, John Adams on, 11-31, 47,
157; Andrew Jackson on, 120-35,
161; Thomas Jefferson on, 48-81,
88, 161
——, in Braintree, Mass., 25
———, colonization of considered: in
Africa, 54, 68, 71; in Brazil, 65; in
Santo Domingo, 64-65, 70-71; in
Sierra Leone, 64, 65; in South
America, 54, 64; in West Indies,
52, 64
——, prospects for in heaven, Andrew
Jackson on, 126

STUDIES IN AMERICAN HISTORY

MOUTON · PUBLISHERS · THE HAGUE

STUDIES IN EUROPEAN HISTORY

MOUTON · PUBLISHERS · THE HAGUE